THE
ULTIMATE
SALES
REVOLUTION

SELL DIFFERENTLY.
CHANGE THE WORLD.

Chase—

May the insights and inspiration in this book support your continued growth and success!

Wishing you great joy and fulfillment in your work and life!

Steve Lishansky

PRAISE FOR *THE ULTIMATE SALES REVOLUTION*

MARC WAYSHAK
Bestselling author of *Game Plan Selling*; Expert Sales Strategist

"Steve Lishansky has changed the game of selling altogether. Not only does his approach help you win more sales, but those sales will be far larger than you ever imagined possible. This book shows you how to work with clients to go from being a 'me too' vendor to their Indispensable Partner in success."

LOUIS NOORDEN
President, The Hire NetWork Inc

"I wish this book was written 30 years ago when I first started The Hire Net.Work Inc. I shudder to think of the time I could have saved developing executive relationships with Fortune 100 companies. This book is a great inspiration and an accelerator for every one of us involved in every level of sales and marketing."

SUZI POMERANTZ, MT, MCC,
CEO, Innovative Leadership International;
Best Selling Author of *Seal the Deal*

"The Ultimate Sales Revolution *is the most important book on business development you will ever read. In fact, get rid of all your other tomes on sales and marketing and get this one! It doesn't matter what business you are in, you will accelerate and amplify your success and your organization's success with these critical distinctions and powerful practices. This is your roadmap for how to get the best possible client relationships and maximum competitive advantage."*

JOE MECHLINSKI
CEO, EntreQuest Inc.; Sales and Leadership Expert

"Steve Lishansky provides the perfect demonstration of how, and why, the world of sales really needs a revolution – and he's the best person I know to lead that revolution. This book is a true treasure trove of strategy and information, supported by an undeniable passion and heart for business and building exceptional relationships. His approach is not only straight-forward and manageable – it's a true and proven recipe for success."

LINDA STEWART
CEO, Innovation Associates

"This book will truly revolutionize the way you think about selling. To reframe what you do from selling to facilitating clarity about what is most important to your clients is a wonderful new way to optimize your relationship with clients. This ultimately translates to better results for the clients – and for you! If selling is a part of your business (and it should be for everyone), this is a must read!"

MITCHELL STEVKO
CEO, SuccessfulGenius.com and TheSleepCompanion.com

"The strategies in this book are the rocket fuel to your next level of high value relationship success! Steve Lishansky is a true genius and master of creating successful sales relationships. His book teaches you how to connect at the highest level of values and what is most important to your client. This is one of the most important business books you will ever read – and one you'll refer to frequently until you've mastered these skills."

JASON PAPPAS
Managing Partner and Co-Founder, Antson Capital Partners

"As someone who practiced, managed, trained and taught sales most of my career I was blown away when I read Steve's book. Steve has never ceased to amaze me with his ability make the complex understandable and effective. The Ultimate Sales Revolution shows you how to master sales better, faster, and far more efficiently. Highly recommended!"

HUW JONES
Senior Global Brand Director, Novartis Pharmaceuticals

"The process of sales is part science and part art. Steve helps us navigate through this world with expertise, insight and conviction. This is a must read for every sales professional."

BARRI RAFFERTY
CEO North America, Ketchum (division of Omnicom)

"Do your clients get exceptional value from doing business with you? Steve Lishansky reconstructs what "sales" should be, and turns an often intimidating process into one of adding immense value for clients. His

training shifted our agency's focus on sales and transformed it to building relationships, value and trust."

JANE DEUBER
CEO, The Virtual Academy Builder; Entrepreneurial Growth Strategist

"This book gives us an insightful window into how business must be done today – and for years to come. This is your best source for any salesperson, leader, or business change agent who is looking to be more successful in the marketplace, and push the boundaries of excellence and innovation. If you are looking to build a culture of organizational and sales excellence, The Ultimate Sales Revolution *shows you the way to make it happen."*

MARK BONCHECK
Founder, thinkORBIT and SHIFT Academy

"Every aspect of business is undergoing profound disruption and accelerating change. We need to rethink our approach to sales in order to compete and win. In The Ultimate Sales Revolution, *Steve Lishansky gives us a roadmap for sales in the 21st century. Selling is no longer about pushing products and promoting benefits. Customers are now co-creators, and salespeople need to be indispensable and collaborative partners. Steve shows us not just what to do, but how to think. This is must reading for anyone looking to shift their business to the next level."*

ZSUZSA NOVAK
Global Impact and Branding Expert

I must admit that I've been avoiding sales as much as I could – until I read The Ultimate Sales Revolution. *It shows how to build partnerships rooted in a foundation of trust, rapport and long-term results. With Steve Lishansky's proven, integrity driven, win-win methodology, you have the blueprint for outstanding high-value communication, client relationships – and success.*

BASIL DENNO
Vice President Sales, Novo Nordisk

"Steve's approach to selling is spot on and a must to succeed for any organization. In today's business environment, you must become a trusted partner – one that understands the clients' business and what

is most important to them. This leads to building trust, increases their willingness to give you time, makes for outstanding long-term relation-ships, and ultimately increases sales. This approach is the foundation for creating great Customer Experience."

NEAL TRICARICO
Vice President Sales, Search Optics; Founder, Sales Growth Inc.

The Sales Industry is going through significant transition, and success will be even greater for those who learn to navigate this new landscape well. The Ultimate Sales Revolution is your must-have road map to deliver the results that matter most to your clients. Steve Lishansky's strategies have changed the trajectory of my career and life. Now, with The Ultimate Sales Revolution, everyone else has access to growing your sales impact, value and success, and improving your career and life

JESSE KIM
Senior Director of Sales, Oracle

"Steve is one of the most inspiring professionals in the field of sales. He is a master at taking something as complex as sales, and making it simple to understand and be far more successful at. This is a must read for anyone seriously committed to success in sales."

CYNTHIA CARPENTER
Vice President Business Products, Charter Communications

"High impact leaders, regardless of their function, will benefit from Steve's wisdom on creating high value relationships."

DAVID ROHLANDER
Best-selling author of *The CEO Code*;
Leadership and Communication Expert

"This universally applicable, impeccable system Steve outlines and clarifies in The Ultimate Sales Revolution *is a must read, for both sales-people and every executive who wants to have greater success dealing with others. Masterfully done!"*

THE
ULTIMATE
SALES
REVOLUTION

SELL DIFFERENTLY.
CHANGE THE WORLD.

STEVE LISHANSKY

THE INSTITUTE FOR SALES INNOVATION

Advantage®

Published by Advantage, Charleston, South Carolina.
Member of Advantage Media Group.

ADVANTAGE is a registered trademark and the Advantage colophon is a trademark of Advantage Media Group, Inc.

Printed in the United States of America.

ISBN: 978-1-59932-551-4
LCCN: 2015940478

Book design by Megan Elger.

This publication is designed to provide accurate and authoritative information in regard to the subject matter covered. It is sold with the understanding that the publisher is not engaged in rendering legal, accounting, or other professional services. If legal advice or other expert assistance is required, the services of a competent professional person should be sought.

Advantage Media Group is proud to be a part of the Tree Neutral® program. Tree Neutral offsets the number of trees consumed in the production and printing of this book by taking proactive steps such as planting trees in direct proportion to the number of trees used to print books. To learn more about Tree Neutral, please visit **www.treeneutral.com**. To learn more about Advantage's commitment to being a responsible steward of the environment, please visit **www.advantagefamily.com/green**

Advantage Media Group is a publisher of business, self-improvement, and professional development books and online learning. We help entrepreneurs, business leaders, and professionals share their Stories, Passion, and Knowledge to help others Learn & Grow. Do you have a manuscript or book idea that you would like us to consider for publishing? Please visit **advantagefamily.com** or call **1.866.775.1696**.

DEDICATION

To my wife Terri
And children Julie, Jenn, Dave and Harry
You inspire and motivate me more than you can imagine
With your love, passion for life, and caring for others.

CONTENTS

INTRODUCTION

"The mere formulation of a problem is far more often essential than its solution, which may be merely a matter of mathematical or experimental skill. To raise new questions, new possibilities, to regard old problems from a new angle requires creative imagination and marks real advances in science."

—ALBERT EINSTEIN

How did we get here:

- [ ] Where high-level salespeople and professional services providers call themselves anything but salespeople...

- [ ] Where prospects and clients don't value salespeople – in fact, they act resentful, defensive, or even offensive when having to deal with salespeople...

- [ ] Where the profession of sales – as significant and critical as it is to business – is the butt of jokes, resentment, and terribly low levels of respect...

You, whether you are a salesperson or must deal with salespeople, deserve a much higher level of respect, understanding, and value in the sales process.

Warning: *This is not your typical sales book.* It is *not* going to teach you yet another sales process for closing deals. It is *not* going to provide you with the "secrets" to negotiating with clients so you get more yeses and fewer nos. It is *not* going to tell you how to perfect your elevator pitch, fact find, or probe your prospects more effectively. All those things describe the way sales is currently practiced.

No. This is a book about revolutionizing sales.

Why revolution? Because *the way sales is practiced today is fundamentally wrong, outdated, and so disreputable that no one wants to be called a salesperson*. One of the greatest days in my career happened when I realized I didn't need to walk into a meeting with a client or prospect armed with all the answers and the classic sales techniques. What I found liberating, empowering, and, best of all, *far more effective* was to do something totally different than sell what I had. Instead, I became **a facilitator of what was most important to that client**.

In this book, you will learn why being a facilitator of what is most important to someone builds the ultimate relationship that every single person, in sales and beyond, needs to have – *because it leads to massively better results* – for the client and the salesperson. You will come to understand why it is so critically important to engage in every relationship by facilitating clarity about what really matters to the other person.

Let me start by giving you an example of what I mean.

A number of years ago, I was working as an executive coach and consultant with smaller, entrepreneurial companies. Through a friend, I got an opportunity to speak with a contact inside a multibillion-dollar financial services firm. This friend had previously worked for the company's head of training in their Information Technology (IT) group and suggested that I talk with this contact to see if he could introduce me to somebody on the sales side of the business.

So I called this guy. He had scheduled just five minutes to talk to me, and when he answered the phone, he literally said to me: "Tell me what you do so I know who to refer you to." Just like that. In rapid-fire delivery. But instead of launching into a pitch about what I do, I started with this: "Rather than give you a laundry list of what I do, please talk about your top two challenges, and I can share with you how we might address those?"

This head of training then proceeded to tell me about some of the biggest challenges his IT group was having. I asked him questions, but he did most of the talking. When he was done, I told him a little bit about how I would approach the problems he was facing. The conversation lasted 15 minutes, at the end of which time he said, "Wait a minute. We need this."

Less than a week later, I was sitting in the offices of this Fortune 500 company with this guy's boss, who was the number-two person in their IT group of 450 people. Just like before, we started talking about what his biggest challenges and opportunities were. He said to me: "Here is our situation. We used to own a piece of the budgets of every division within this company. We would walk in and say, 'I understand you've got $3.2 million. Let me tell you how we're going to spend it for you.' Now, because of a recent reorganization, not only do those now-independent business units *not* have to spend money on IT, if they do spend money, they can choose to buy services from outside the company instead of dealing with us. Right now, 48 percent of our clients are complaining that our prices are too high. Oh, and we can't sustain our group on the internal transfer price, so it's a real crisis. We've been given just one year to fix this. So, we're looking for a three- or four-day training on how to market our IT services to these clients who no longer have to give us their business."

It was a critical situation, and knowing training as I do, my first question to him was: "Have you ever had a three- or four-day training that had sustainable and successful results of this magnitude?"

He said, "No."

So I said, "And what is the cost of failure if you have the best possible three- or four-day training, but it doesn't end up producing your critical results?"

He said, "We're out of business in a year."

Having helped him create a critical realization, I said, "Well then, I'd suggest a different approach."

That opened up a whole new conversation, and we went on to talk about what his group really needed, which was for his people to stop talking about their IT expertise and start focusing on helping their clients achieve their most important results. Then I spent just 15 minutes proposing a different solution than what he had asked for. Instead of just a training program that lasted a few days, I suggested one that would take place in 20 sessions over six months. I also suggested one-on-one coaching for each of their top client relationship managers, which was 60 people in all, to help them apply the information they were learning in their work with clients. I explained that this would be important because, up to now, their people had been the experts. All they had to do was tell their clients what they were going to do with their IT budgets. Now, they would have to treat those people like real clients and help them see how to improve and accelerate their critical results with their IT investments. That was going to be a radical change in perspective, approach, and execution that would require new skills and perspective.

After an hour and five minutes, the boss stood up, shook my hand, and said: "If my people could do with their clients what you just did with me, we'd have no problems."

Five days later I was ushered in to meet with the CIO. He talked to me for just ten minutes before turning to the head of training and his boss I'd met with. He said to them, "Guys, I'm going to go with your decision." Up to that point I thought I was just a finalist, but they both pointed at me and said, "We want him."

That was the beginning of a seven-year relationship with the company, where every six months we would renew our commitment to achieve the results that were most critical for them. And the results were remarkable. When we started out, 48 percent of their clients were complaining about high prices. At the end of the year, they surveyed again. We had raised the price of their services by 50 percent – and reduced complaints about pricing to just 12 percent of their clients. The year after that, the IT group won the award for most outstanding client satisfaction in the enterprise for that Fortune 500 company. That's unheard of when it comes to IT groups (no one I know has ever heard of another case of it happening). Finally, when this multibillion dollar company was bought by a company almost five times their size, the guy who had originally wanted me – and who had since been promoted to CIO – ended up becoming CIO of the parent company's largest division. Why? Because people in his company loved dealing with him. He had learned to be an Indispensable Partner in their success.

So, what was supposed to begin as a five-minute phone call turned into an hour-and-five minute discussion, which launched a seven-year, immensely valuable and successful relationship. And the runner-up, who had been competing for the same business but didn't get it, had spent six days with this client over the prior few months before I came in. In all that time, he hadn't managed to convince them that he knew enough about them and the issues they were facing to instill confidence. Because if he had, I wouldn't have even made it through the door.

What was the key to winning this business? They were not being sold what I had. I didn't talk about what I could do. The big value I provided right up front was in helping the client get away from what they thought they wanted and to get clear about their most important results. Once the critical results were clear, then I could help them find a way to achieve those results. That's how they came to see the powerful potential of having me as an Indispensable Partner in their success.

This book is about showing you how you too can become an Indispensable Partner in your prospects' and clients' success. Contained in these Indispensable Partner principles, perspectives, and practices are revolutionary ways to be highly successful in sales that are – in total – markedly different than the way almost everyone practices sales today.

ABOUT ME

You might be wondering at this point: Who is this guy to be calling for a sales revolution?

I have two things in my favor. Number one, I've been selling my entire life. My first experience with sales was at the age of five. I was living on an Air Force base in Mississippi, where mistletoe grew in the local trees. At Christmas time, I went door-to-door selling it for five cents. I had my first taste of sales success right away. After all, who was going to turn down a cute five-year-old selling mistletoe for a nickel at Christmas time? The funny thing is I grew up Jewish, but it didn't matter.

Since then I have done everything from run my own lawn mowing company as a teenager (I made the equivalent of about $40 an hour in today's dollars, which wasn't too shabby for a 13-year-old) to starting my own toy company, to selling services for top companies in a variety of fields, to, in 1992, founding my current companies, The Institute for Sales Innovation and Optimize International. Both companies focus on rapidly accelerating and expanding the results that sales people, leaders and executive teams achieve, including building cultures of excellence and high performance.

The second thing I have going for me is that I've studied with some of the world's great geniuses, masters, and mentors who taught me to really understand human dynamics and phenomena. What has always fascinated me since I was young were the twin questions: What makes people do what they do? What makes some people successful and others not? Some people who don't have great intelligence are very successful, and some brilliant people don't achieve anywhere near what you would expect. I have spent decades searching out and understanding powerful answers and insights to these questions.

In the course of my study, research, and experience with thousands of top professionals, leaders, and executives from more than 40 countries, I developed some powerful universal principles. Studying and applying the practices of phenomenology – the study of what actually happens (versus the story about what happens) – led me to develop some core insights into how human beings function, behave, think, and make their decisions. I have taught exactly the same principles to groups in Beijing, Barcelona, Boston, and every place in between, and they've proven to be effective all around the world. At the most fundamental level, **suc-**

cessful people differentiate themselves from others by figuring out how to provide outstanding value to somebody or some group.

In this age of extraordinary innovation, getting clear about what people want – when *they* don't even know what they really want – is the basis of success for so many companies and products. As Henry Ford once said: "If I had asked people what they wanted, they would have told me faster horses."

Among the successes that came from creatively delivering great value to people are Walt Disney's Disneyland and Disney World parks; Sony's Walkman portable music player; Apple's iPod, iPhone, and iPad consumer electronics revolutions; the ubiquity of Google's search engines; eBay's open-to-everyone, online marketplace; and Amazon's being the place to purchase almost anything you could want through your computer or phone. What separates these great successes from other great ideas that never went anywhere is not just the creation of something new and wonderful but the ability to help people see the value for themselves and their lives. **Where people find meaningful value, massive opportunity exists.**

With this understanding and my background in phenomenology and human dynamics, I started looking at what makes the biggest difference in sales. I sell my services like anyone else, and my competition can be the big name consulting companies. Yet I do a good job of winning against them. The valuable distinction I make is that, when I meet a client, I don't talk about me and my history of success in business. I facilitate with them – getting them clear about what is most important to them – and connecting them to their most critical results in a way that nobody else seems to do as consistently.

From the very first conversation, the focus and communication is on **getting the clients clear about what are their most important and valuable results**. As you will learn, most of the time they are not clear or focused on what would ultimately be most critical to their own success. It is profoundly powerful to see how **a deep trust and connection gets generated when you help clients shift their focus from a premature and inadequate request to their most meaningful and valuable results**. This kind of facilitation and trust building moves smart clients to say, "I want to work with this person."

This kind of demonstration of value is so powerful that today, up to a quarter of my clients hire me *without asking what it costs*. Isn't that exactly the sort of position of trust and respect that any sales professional today wants to be in?

What is it worth to you to demonstrate so much value to your client that they consider it so immensely important to work with you – that price is a secondary issue?

WHO CAN BENEFIT FROM THIS BOOK?

The answer to that is simple: Anybody who deals with other human beings.

In this book you will learn the universal basis for success in any relationship with another human being – in any context. It could be a friend, a spouse, a family member, a service provider, a vendor, or an employee. Everyone can benefit from these principles and practices. For the top-notch professional service providers and salespeople with whom I work the most, the ones who have hundreds of thousands or millions of dollars at stake in a deal or project, this is more than beneficial – it is critical. As you'll see in the coming pages, if you're one of these top-notch professionals, you need to be able to differentiate yourself in this way, to make sure that the clients trust you to take care of what is most important to them. That is one of the essential foundations for both winning business and being highly successful in your engagements. And you're going to prove this from the very first time you talk with them by keeping the focus on and connecting them to what is really most important to them.

If you're reading this book, you're probably already very successful. You deal at a very high level with your clients. But you probably also know you're losing more business than you should, and you don't know exactly why. When your competitors are beating you, it is not just because they've offered a lower price. When you are being forced to offer lower prices to win business, it means you're being commoditized, getting paid for the amount of activity you do and not the value you provide. As you'll soon learn, **the ultimate key to success in winning business – as well as getting paid what you should – is to get paid for the value your clients get**.

ABOUT THIS BOOK

This book is structured in two parts. In Part I, The Revolution, you will understand what is wrong with how sales is currently practiced by almost everyone today. You will also see why these sales practices are not working well enough and the alternative that is massively better for all parties – salespeople, clients, and their companies. You will be introduced to the keys that make the difference in building massive impact, value, and results.

In Part II, Successfully Implementing The Ultimate Sales Revolution, you will learn, step by step, exactly how to create the perspective and practice sales in this new way. There are a lot of people out there who talk about client focus, client relationships, and helping the client get to what they need, but nobody has what I call a **universally impeccable system that is based on proven principles of human dynamics.**

This book is going to explain the steps to outstanding communication, which is the critical building block for the best possible relationships. These high-value relationships are what lead to the greatest impact, value, and results for your clients – and for you.

While sales is the main focus of this book, it is important to understand that this book is based on universal principles of impeccable communication and relationship building that will lead to the maximization of value in any relationship. Throughout the book you will also find my Ultimate Sales Axioms, which are powerful principles that support your success in this new way of thinking, selling, and succeeding.

Once you understand this revolutionary new approach and master the process laid out for you, you will find that your sales experience is far more successful, far simpler, and far more personally satisfying than ever before. Most importantly, you will find that you are able to produce dramatic results at levels that are almost hard to imagine, yet which will seem so natural to you and your clients.

"The world as we have created it is a process of our thinking.
It cannot be changed without changing our thinking."
—ALBERT EINSTEIN

"When you can do a common thing in an uncommon way, you will command the attention of the world."

—George Washington Carver

PART I

THE REVOLUTION

CHAPTER ONE

WHY IS THE SALES PROCESS SO BROKEN?

*"When you change the way you look at things,
the things you look at change."*

—MAX PLANCK, Nobel Prize winner in Physics

When speaking to groups of sales professionals, I often start by posing a series of basic, yet often unasked, questions:

☐ Why is it that no one wants to call a prospect and say, "I'm a salesman," or "I'm a saleswoman"?

☐ Why is it that no one loves the idea of talking to salespeople?

☐ Why is it that salespeople are among the least admired and lowest rated professions – at the same low level as Congress?

☐ Why is it that every salesperson seems to have a euphemism for what they do? People's business cards don't say "salesperson" anymore; instead they say "business development specialist," "client relationship manager," "producer," or similar terms attempting to divert prospects and clients from having to deal with another salesperson.

The successful, high-level sales professionals I work with every day know exactly what I'm talking about when I ask them these questions. The best way to transform this situation is to practice sales principles that eliminate the basis for these unnecessary perceptions.

This situation begs for a high-quality answer to the question: Why are people so resistant to salespeople? When you walk into a meeting with a new prospect or client, isn't there almost always a leeriness or hesitancy right off the bat? Defensiveness? A barrier between you and the person you are looking to serve? There is a nasty obstacle course to be run in the way sales is practiced today, and nobody enjoys it – not the clients and not the salespeople.

The fundamental reason for this is that **sales has become about what a salesperson *does* to the prospect or client**. Sales has become about me against you, regardless of how elegantly it is framed. What do I, as the salesperson (or producer or business development specialist or insert any other euphemism for salesperson here) need to do to get you into my camp? What do I need to do to get you to deal with me and my company? What do I need to do to move you to buy? What do I need to do to convince you, to influence you, to get you to do what *I* want *you* to do? Even if I am doing something that will ultimately benefit the client, the problem is that **no one really wants to have things *done to them.***

That, in a nutshell, is what sales is all about today. When you visit a client, even one with high-level needs and a budget in the millions, it's as if you're automatically pitted against one another. You try to figure out the best way to move the client in a certain direction. Meanwhile, the client knows full well that you're trying to do this, so he's putting up barriers to protect himself. It is a cat-and-mouse game, when **it needs to be a partnership, for the greater good of both the client and the salesperson.**

The fundamental issues with how sales is practiced today are these:

1. **Practically all salespeople today don't know enough about their client's business.**

2. **Practically all salespeople today don't know what their clients really need.**

3. **Most of the time, the clients don't know what is really most important to their ultimate success, either.**

The client is playing the same game as the salesperson, which means **both parties are focused on the wrong things**. And that is the big secret that almost nobody understands about sales as it is practiced today. (More on this soon.)

THE $8 MILLION DISASTER

One of my IT clients told me about their $8 million disaster around a contract for a major hardware and software project. Together with their client, this service provider drew up 100 pages of specifications for the project and estimated delivery in two years. Well, two years turned into three, as happens too often with IT projects. And, as also happens with IT projects, it went over budget – way over budget. In the end, the service provider delivered the specifications that had been drawn up in the beginning. So the client must have been happy, right? Wrong, really wrong.

By the time the project was complete, the client had spent $8 million, only to throw the whole thing in the garbage.

How could this happen? It happened because even though the service provider had ultimately delivered the technical specifications that had been promised, by the time the project finished, the technology had become obsolete, irrelevant, and not useful to their client.

How would you like to work on a major project for three years of your life, invest $8 million, and then throw it away? You wouldn't like it. And neither did this client, or all of those talented technical experts who saw their hours, weeks, months, and years of effort get thrown away.

The real question is: Who is responsible when something like that happens? Is it the client, who asked for more than 100 pages of specifications that he wanted the service provider to deliver? Or is it the service provider, who was supposed to be the expert in this area? Obviously, the client blamed their IT experts, and you can bet that relationship was never the same again.

Whose responsibility is it to make things work when clients are demanding and insistent, and top professional salespeople and service providers agree and acquiesce to something they don't have certainty and confidence in? Saying yes to a client who is asking for something that does not have clear, obvious, and mea-sureable value and impact is creating a path to failure – regardless of how much that client demands and claims to know what they want.

Sadly, stories like this one are too common in business today, and it is symptomatic of how sales has gone very wrong. I'm sure there were people within that IT company who said to themselves and each other, "Well, we did what they asked us to, so how can they blame us?" But they can blame you. And they will blame you. Because you took their money and, regardless of anything that you did, you didn't provide **the most important and essential outcome of all – real value to the client**.

Regardless of how much clients demand and insist, **agreeing to something that does not have real, meaningful, measureable, and significant value is perpetuating the weakest practices of traditional sales**. That is trying to get closer to the client by agreeing to what they say they want, and trying to prove your worth by doing the things they ask for – even when the requests you so "nobly" agree to do not generate valuable and important results for them.

THE PROBLEM WITH "LET ME TELL YOU WHAT I DO"

One of the big ways in which sales has gone wrong is that salespeople today are often out there trying to win clients and business by virtue of how much information they can provide: "Let me tell you about what we do. Let me tell you why it would be great for you. Let me tell you why it is better than our competitors. Let me tell you with whom we've worked in the past. Let me tell you how well we've done for our other clients like you."

Here is the fundamental problem with that approach: **When someone is buying high-level professional services, most of the time he can't tell the difference between you and your top five competitors – and certainly not on a technical basis**.

Think about your own decision-making process in choosing a doctor, for example. When you need to have surgery, do you ask the doctor to explain his expertise in this area? Do you ask him what tools he's going to use to perform the surgery? Do you ask him to walk you through, step by step, how he'll be performing the surgery? Of course you don't. What would you do with a surgeon who begins by going into this kind of detail about what he knows and what he is going to do?

What you want is to feel like you can **trust him or her to take care of your best interests – even when you cannot define what**

they are. You do know the single most important outcome – that you recover your full health. **What you want most is confidence and comfort that this person understands, cares about, and can be trusted to deliver on your most important results.**

This is the same way you hire other technical experts whose expertise you are not in a position to evaluate. These could include your accountant, lawyer, dentist, financial planner, investment manager, architect, general contractor, auto mechanic, wealth management advisor, consultant, or any other professional whose skills are beyond your technical understanding. Do you really want them to explain their education, tools, technical decision-making process, or how many people like you they have worked with?

What we really want is for them to help us get clear about what the best and most important results we could achieve in their area of expertise would be – and then get us those results. The people we hire are the ones who we feel "get us" best, the ones we feel care about our best interests and will put these first as they deliver our important results. Building our confidence, trust, and respect in their attention to and ability to take care of what is most important to us is the primary reason we want to work with them. This is the fundamental basis upon which human beings make their most important choices. This is especially true when we don't even possess the ability to fully evaluate their professional and technical expertise. We have to trust them – and earning that trust is a critical platform for success.

Another example has to do with how technology is often marketed these days. I recently saw an ad comparing Apple's new iPhone to a Samsung model in terms of their specifications. In terms of pure specs, the Samsung appeared to be the faster of the two, but does the average consumer really understand the difference between what a 2.7 gigahertz processor can do versus a 1.8 gigahertz processor? No, they cannot. What is missing is a discussion of what important results this technology can deliver for you. How well can it make your life better in the ways that you really care about? How well does it improve the way you work, make your life easier, create more fun – or even improve the overall functioning of your phone? Unless you are clear about what results you want most from your phone, you can easily be taken in by technical details, like size or processing speed, that sound sexy and good – even when they don't deliver what you need most.

And yet, so many salespeople today spend their time trying to differentiate themselves on the basis of what they do. Too many of them get hung up on details, activities, processes, and specifications. While that may be common in traditional sales, **the best way to build the critical confidence, trust, and respect in you as the provider of choice is to demonstrate that you understand what the clients really care about most.** The caveat here is that **very often the clients are not clear about what they really need or would benefit from the most. This gap between what they think they want or are looking at, and what would produce the most important and valuable results for them, is what The Ultimate Sales Revolution addresses best.**

To give just one example of this, years ago a friend was responsible for purchasing desktop computers for a Fortune 100 corporation. This is going back a lot of years, because this was the first time they were going to have desktop computers throughout the company. There were four groups that came in to present to him.

Digital Equipment, working together with Microsoft, was far and away the leader in terms of the sheer quality of their technology at that time. But they were the first ones eliminated. Dead last in his rating of the four contenders in terms of pure technology was IBM, and they won the business. Why?

Based on pure technical specifications, Digital Equipment would have won the business. However, mere technical superiority was seriously deficient relative to the ultimate result required. Here is what IBM did: they honed in on the real concerns driving the decision, which was not who had the most sophisticated or even the best-priced computers. The client's real issue was how to get their people to use this new technology. Otherwise, they'd be spending many tens of millions of dollars for nothing, because putting a computer on everyone's desk is meaningless unless people use it appropriately to advance the company's needs and outcomes. The group that best understood that was IBM. They understood that the key to success was not the speed of their computers but rather their ability to integrate the company's systems and help people learn to and want to use their computers. IBM demonstrated that they understood the real issue by offering the company the best implementation support and training.

When Digital Equipment was eliminated, here is what the salesperson actually said: "Can I come in and tell my story again?" *Tell my story again.* What would you say to that? Why would anyone want to hear his story? After all, the client had already heard this guy's story and knew he didn't understand the most important results the client's organization needed. That salesman represented the fastest, coolest, and most sophisticated technology at that moment. **What he was missing, which cost him the business, was an understanding of the critical results his prospect needed.**

What the Digital Equipment salesperson offered was the classic "We are the best" story. Obviously, that's not how you convince, persuade, influence, support, take care of, or become a partner in your client's success. Clients don't need your story. They need you to listen to their story, and far more importantly – understand their most important needs. **Demonstrating that they can trust you to take care of their most critical outcomes and deliver the results that are most valuable to them is your greatest differentiator in sales. This is what builds the trust, respect, and openness that mark the most successful sales relationships**. (By the way, that's the whole point of the process that is outlined in this Part II of this book.)

THE CASE FOR REVOLUTION

It is not just that revolution is needed in the way we practice sales. It is that revolution happens whether we like it or not. So you can be part of it, or you can fail and die.

The revolution is here. The world has already changed. As a result, we have to rethink the entire sales game because the way sales is currently practiced simply isn't working well enough. Too much effort is being put in for too little result. And no one seems very happy with the relationship – neither the clients nor the sales professionals themselves. If they were, salespeople wouldn't be trying to hide the fact that they're in sales by calling themselves anything but a salesperson, and clients would welcome the opportunity to speak with someone they believe could provide outstanding value, impact, and results to them.

The world in which we do business today is more competitive than ever. There is more information available than ever. It is easier to find out who a person is and what they've done than ever before. All this means that it is a lot harder to deceive clients, but it is very easy to overload them. And this is a phenomenon that's affecting our entire culture, not just salespeople. Technology has accelerated the pace of activity, but the problem is that too few have paused to consider the implications of what they're doing. **The whole world has changed, and we're still doing what we've always done, but we're doing it faster**. That's just foolishness.

That's why 20 percent of the Fortune 500 has disappeared every ten years over the past three decades, either by merger or dissolution. Remember who the biggest retailer in the world was in the 1920s, '30s, '40s? Woolworths. And it doesn't exist anymore. What was the largest retailer in the world in the 1990s? It was K-Mart. They have been in bankruptcy and teetering on the brink of extinction. General Motors was the biggest and one of the most valuable companies on the planet not so long ago. No longer in the top 20 in revenue, nor in the top 150 in value, they have been through bankruptcy and are working to reinvent themselves and solidify their future as a company.

By comparison, it is worth remembering that the beginning of the Internet boom is considered to be August 1995, when Netscape went public. Yet today, some of the most valuable companies in the world are innovative technology companies, like Google, Alibaba, Facebook, and Priceline, which did not even exist then. Of course, the story of Apple is a brilliant story of reinvention, having gone from near bankruptcy and being declared dead and irrelevant to being the most valued company in the history of the world. What they did was reinvent the world of music listening and mobile communications – and their computers continue to lead all others in terms of ease of use and quality of design. In each of these areas, they were not the first to do what they did. They did it better and easier for their customers. They created wow experiences that gave people what they did not even know they wanted

– and which they continue to desire and buy with a fervor that very few products or companies generate.

You can be on the successful side of this wave of sales revolution, or you can continue to perpetuate practices that have led to disdain for sales by so many, including those who are in sales.

Even the very fundamental definitions of major areas are changing. For instance, the definition of economics has changed, but not enough people have recognized it. For many decades, economics was defined as the study of the allocation of scarce resources. Can you tell me the scarce resource at Google, Microsoft, LinkedIn, Facebook, Twitter, or even Apple?

One reason old thinking persists is because too many of us today have overpacked to-do lists. We jump on the "to-do list hamster wheel" and, spinning like crazy, don't take the time to consider, rethink, and recalibrate where we are actually going or what we are ultimately trying to achieve that would be most meaningful and valuable. Somebody who is under a lot of pressure to deliver some result in a very short timeframe is not thinking about where the world is going to be in the next 6, 12, or 24 months. Too many times, they are putting too much effort into doing something that won't even move them toward a short-term, meaningful result.

If you keep doing, doing, doing, without consideration for what the real results need to be, you end in deep do-do (doo-doo). Unfortunately, those are the people who get left behind in the long run. And that's certainly true when it comes to sales. Many people are doing too much to try to prove they are good and worth working with instead of helping clients make sure that what they are focusing on will provide real results that matter.

Another key element driving today's business climate is companies thinking short term. Most public companies are judged by their quarterly results. Those of us who have worked with technology companies know that in the last few weeks of their quarter – and even more so at the end of their fiscal years – every salesperson is pushing like crazy to get deals done and hit their quarterly targets. They all get measured and bonused based on how they did for the quarter. So, rather than build long-term, meaningful relationships with clients that work over time, salespeople are pressured to get results now. But how does that make sense for the client? And how does that help you build successful long-term relationships, ones that are worth a lot more in the long run?

This is not what the clients want today. And clients, more than ever, have more information and choices. **What they want and what they need is for their best interests to be the fundamental focus for the salesperson**. Remember the example of the $8 million, three-year disaster that resulted in so much wasted time and resources as well as the demoralization of the team? Sometimes we have to save clients from themselves and from poor decision-making. And what better way to demonstrate our value – even before we sell them anything?

That's what this book is all about – maximizing real, meaningful value for your clients and building the kind of relationship that allows you to ultimately maximize the valuable results for yourself and for your company. What you are going to learn is how to help clients get clear about what is most important to them, how to connect that to what is most valuable to them and their organization, and make sure that you understand each other in terms of what the quality, impact, and value of those results really is worth.

CHAPTER TWO

THE THREE SOURCES OF MISCOMMUNICATION

*"Discovery consists of seeing what everybody has
seen and thinking what nobody has thought."*

—ALBERT VON SZENT-GYORGYI, Nobel Prize winner in Medicine

One of the areas of my expertise that my clients find **most valuable is a fundamental understanding of human dynamics – why exactly people do what they do – and how that influences communication, decision-making, relationship-building, sales, and even leadership**. Every top professional must have a strong understanding of the driving forces of communication. One of the big problems with sales today is that salespeople fail to understand how to effectively communicate and fail to recognize how often miscommunication is happening. This has a harmful, if not a disastrous, impact on their relationships with their clients.

Some of the ideas in this book were developed when I was working with a group of leaders at one of the world's leading engineering firms. They knew they were giving away dollars and free business in the hope that it would buy them better client relationships. This went on because most of their engineering projects were very sophisticated, and when working on such complex projects, things come up that no one could have planned for. In the interest of trying to please and keep their clients happy, they would say, "Don't worry about it. We'll make the changes you need, and then we'll make the adjustments at the end." Normally you'd go through the process of writing up a change order and getting it approved by the client, but that process could take time, which would slow the project down. Trying to prove they were nice people with the client's interests at heart, their people would say, "Let's just go ahead and do what we need to do, and we'll take care of the formalities later."

This was happening so often that the company ended up with $8 million in questionable collections because at the end of the project, many clients would protest the additional but undocumented costs. They would say, "Hey, what are these extras you added to the bill? They weren't part of our original agreement, you didn't get a change order for them, so we're not paying for them."

The people at this engineering firm had good intentions. They were trying to be easy to work with and to keep their projects on track. But what they were really doing was trying to buy relationships by giving away business.

I got them to rethink their approach to relationship building and taught them how to deal effectively with their clients. When we first started working with them, some of their people were wondering, "I'm a top notch leader of great engineers, so why should I care about relationships and communication? That is not my area of interest or expertise."

I asked them, "What is your biggest challenge?"

They said, "Our clients."

So I asked, "What is the problem with your clients?"

"They don't communicate well. They get angry. They're a pain in the neck," they said.

So I said to them, "At the most basic level, there are only three *sources* of miscommunication. If you know what they are and you know how to handle them, you'll never have a problem with a client that you can't manage."

Their responses to my question, "What is the problem with your clients," are classics. They're the kind I get all the time when I ask people this question. In fact, if you ask professional service providers what their biggest challenge is, the answer you're *most likely* to get is: "My clients don't communicate clearly." I know this because I've asked it of thousands of top-notch sales, marketing, technical, and managerial professionals all over the world, in a wide variety of industries, over more than 23 years.

Why don't clients communicate clearly? Boiling it down to the simplest and most universal basis, I claim that there are only three reasons for miscommunication. I call these The Three Sources of Miscommunication. What would you guess they are – before I reveal them on the next page?

WHAT WOULD YOU GUESS ARE THE THREE SOURCES OF MISCOMMUNICATION?

1—

2—

3—

SOURCE OF MISCOMMUNICATION #1: YOU

The first cause of miscommunication is YOU. As I said, having worked with thousands of people from more than 40 countries around the world, I've had the opportunity to ask top-notch professionals from every continent (except Antarctica) this question: "What percentage of the time are you a highly effective communicator?"

All around the world, the responses are consistently the same. The responses almost always range between 60 to 80 percent of the time – so 70 percent is the average. What is the obvious implication of that? The implication is that **30 percent of the time, when miscommunication happens, *you* are the source.**

SOURCE OF MISCOMMUNICATION #2: THEM

The second cause of miscommunication is THEM. Again, I've had a chance to pose this question to professionals from all over the world: "What percentage of the time is the initial request a prospect or client gives you directly connected to what is ultimately most important, critical, and valuable to them?"

The answer is most often between 10 to 20 percent of the time. That means that 80 to 90 percent of the time, your clients are not telling you what is most critical and most important to them. And this is not because they're hiding the information from you. It happens because they haven't thought it through well. They're not focused on what really matters but rather on what has grabbed their attention – or the attention of their boss – at that moment. Their lack of clarity about what is most important to them means you run the risk of doing immense amounts of work to produce something they asked for – even though it is not very important, meaningful, or valuable. That is dangerous, akin to walking into a trap that will cause you great harm.

What is the implication of this? **If you do exactly what your client asks you to do as their service provider, then 80 to 90 percent of the time, you will miss the opportunity to deliver optimal value to them**. Remember that three-year, $8 million IT project I told you about earlier in this section? That's exactly what happened there. The service provider did everything that was asked of them, and at the end of the project, the client trashed it. And when the project you've completed for your client doesn't work out very well, who is the client going to blame? You may say, "I did exactly what you asked me to do, on time, on budget, and according to all the specifications." To which the client will likely respond, "But that's not what I really needed. What did I hire you for anyway? You're supposed to be the expert, and you didn't get me what I really needed."

That's a pretty staggering thing to think about in terms of your own business, so I'm going to say it again: If you do exactly what your client asks you to do, then 80 to 90 percent of the time you will fail to deliver the most important value. You will miss the opportunity to build a great relationship and demonstrate how good you and your company can be for them. And the client is going to see it as your fault.

SOURCE OF MISCOMMUNICATION #3:
YOU AND THEM TOGETHER

The third cause of miscommunication is YOU and THEM TOGETHER. That means that something gets lost in translation between you and your client when you are communicating together.

To illustrate this idea in my seminars, I get a group of five people together, who usually are on a team that knows each other and works together on a regular basis. I then give them a word that they all use every day. For example, if I were working with a team in the medical field, I might give them the word "patient." Then I'd ask, "What are the first five things that come to mind when I say the word patient?" Everyone writes down the first five things that come to mind. In technology, I might use the word "software" or "technology." For salespeople, I often use the words "client" or "selling," and for leadership teams I use the word "leadership."

A group has one match when all five people have exactly the same word on their list. They can have as many as five matches if all five people have the same five words on their lists. Having done this exercise with more than 1,400 groups of five people, do you know how many times we've had five matches? Never. Four matches? Zero. Three matches? You can probably see the trend emerging here. It is also zero.

Remember, these are people who already know each other and work together dealing with this very basic word that's key to their business. We've done this with people in all sorts of industries, and all over the world, and out of 1,400 groups, do you know how many times we have had even two matches? Exactly twice. And out of that many groups, all five people have had just one single word match a total of fourteen times. Fourteen out of 1,400.

That means people who know each other well don't have the same association with a basic word that they use regularly in their professional work 99 percent of the time. In every case, people obviously know what the word means, yet they don't know what the word means to the people they are regularly working with. **Which**

do you think is more important – knowing what a word means or knowing what the people you are dealing with think it means?

Imagine how out of tune and alignment we must be with our clients, colleagues, and others we communicate with when they are asking us to do something faster, better, or cheaper? How often are you using your definition of "faster," "better," or "cheaper" and missing what that other person really meant? Given that there is so little understanding of other people's meaning of common words among those who work together regularly, you can imagine the possibilities for miscommunication among people who don't know each other very well.

WHY THIS UNDERSTANDING IS CRITICAL

Why does recognizing the critical lessons of the Three Sources of Miscommunication matter when it comes to sales? In the current way sales is practiced, you as the salesperson are in your world, the client is in their world, and together you're trying to find some place to come together and connect. But we know that at least 30 percent of the time you are going to be less than a highly effective communicator with your client. We also know that 90 percent of the time, the client is not telling you what matters most. Quite likely, the client has not fully thought through how what they are asking for is connected to what is ultimately most important for them, their organization, and their clients. And we know that 99 percent of the time, you and the client don't fully understand exactly what each of you really mean.

So if all you're doing is listening to your client and trying to figure out how you fit into their world, you are in what I call "puzzle pieces" mode. You obviously have some capability and value – your puzzle pieces. The client has some gaps in their picture and seems to be looking for someone with the puzzle pieces to fill in these missing spots. This mechanical, fill-in-the-missing-pieces approach is archaic in today's fast-paced, complex, ever-changing, bound-to-encounter-unforeseen-issues business world. This is especially true for high-level professional services providers, although this approach has always been weak at generating the best possible impact, value, and results for clients.

What is required is to really **enter the client's world and assist them in reaching clarity about what are the most important and valuable results that would produce the greatest impact and value**. Your ability to help them elevate their requests to the level of meaningful outcomes dramatically positions you as superior to your competitors. You are proving that you are a worthy partner in their realizing significant value. You are someone they can trust to achieve more of what really matters than they even started out considering.

This repositioning is akin to fundamentally shifting your position with a client. Imagine sitting across from your client, listening to their request, trying to figure out how to move your "pieces" into their puzzle. Anyone reading this book has enough experience to know that this dance can be quite awkward, choppy, and has its share of missteps.

Let's take the Ultimate Sales Revolution approach instead. Move to the other side of the desk – metaphorically at least. **Instead of looking at your client, look at what your client is looking at.** You already know they rarely have thought through the ultimate end results that would be of greatest value and often are asking for steps on the way to those results. If it is not crystal clear to them and you how these stepping-stones lead to the ultimate, high-value destination, you first need to help them connect the dots. As their partner – not their puzzle-fitting salesperson – **help them to make sure that what they are asking for will deliver what they need most**. Facilitate their clarity and focus on what is most important so that the ultimate results are crystal clear to them.

Done well, **this is entirely about them and what they would benefit from most**. At this point in the conversation it has **nothing at all to do with you**, what your company offers, or anything you can do – except helping them get to that ultimate clarity about what is critically most important for them. **Your ability to focus on them and help them elevate their clarity and focus to what would be of greatest impact and value, builds the fundamental foundation of all great relationships: trust that you will take care of their best interests, even when they don't know what those best interests are**. After all, you are proving it right here, in the beginning of your relationship.

Let's go back to how you choose your doctor, lawyer, dentist, investment manager, consultant, or any other top service provider who has skills and technical capabilities that you don't. Do you want the doctor who tells you all about his degrees, number of patients treated, and specialized protocols or the doctor who listens to you and helps you sort out your symptoms so you can feel confident he understands you and can be trusted to help you get healthy again? **In most cases you don't even understand all that he is going to do, but you want to trust that you are being taken care of by this person who has your best interests at heart**.

I often use a simpler analogy of hiring a carpenter to do some work on your kitchen. Which of these two carpenters are you going to hire? The first one comes in with a big black bag. He puts it down and starts pulling out all kinds of tools. He shows you his high-end drills, saws, routers, and other tools you don't even recognize. He attempts to regale you with tales of how rare and unique his tools are and how some are even designed to his specifications to do the things that other carpenters can't do. He tells you about some of the unique installations he has done with some big-name celebrities. After this intensive show and tell, he asks you if it's clear that he is obviously the best choice to do this work?

The second carpenter comes in and also has a big black bag. He doesn't even open it though. He starts out by asking what exactly you are thinking about. He seems very interested and intent on understanding not only what you want done but also how you want it done. He asks about what feel you want your renovated space to have, how you came to decide now is the time to do it, and how much disruption would be acceptable in getting your work done? He wants to know if there are any other considerations you have about this undertaking, the end result, and the best timing for you. He has not even opened his bag yet, but you know this guy knows what he is doing by how clear he helped you get about the process and the end result.

So whom do you hire? Everyone wants the second carpenter, who made it about you and not about him. Everyone wants the doctor, lawyer, consultant, financial advisor, auto mechanic, and every other professional service provider who **shows us that they are there to take care of us and what we really need, rather than "do their thing" to us.**

In the world of sales, your ability to provide value in the form of greater clarity and focus on what is most important to your clients is your single greatest differentiator from your competitors. Do you really believe your clients can evaluate your technical expertise as superior to your top five competitors? That is not how they are choosing. They are choosing the provider who demonstrates the best quality of engagement, contribution to their thinking and clarity, and who they trust to take care of them best.

Are you on their side, helping them see more clearly what would be of greatest value, or are you trying to fit your puzzle pieces into their picture? Becoming a partner in their success – from the first "hello" all the way through to shaking hands and signing the agreement – is the key to their success and yours. The more it is about them and getting them to clarity, the more you are demonstrating your value as a partner. The more it is about you and what you do, the more you are distancing yourself from them – and from understanding what you need to know to deliver real results that matter.

I hope that you are getting an inkling that what also has to change to maximize your ultimate success is the understanding of how effective communication leads to the highest quality of relationship and how that is essential to the development and demonstration of value that elevates you far above all of your competitors. This is how you become the one that clients want, choose, and decide to work with.

MISPLACED PRIORITIES AND DECISION MAKING

We live in a fast-paced world where we're all burdened with too much information and too many activities on our to-do lists. **The most important question every leader, every professional service provider, every salesperson – everybody – needs to ask is: "How do we decide what is worth doing?"** I've been asking successful, high-performing people this question for more than 20 years: "How many of you can do everything on your to-do list?" The answer, around the world, is zero.

We need to remember what we learned in the Three Sources of Miscommunication: most initial requests from clients are not what is most valuable to them. If we can't do everything we're being asked to do, and clients ask you to do things that aren't what is most valuable to them, then how do you decide what is worth doing?

Most people answer, "Whoever screams the loudest," or, "Whoever has the highest position," or, "Whatever I can actually do easily." These are all good ways to fail.

You want to make decisions in the most intelligent and effective ways. When you want to be highly successful, **you always focus on and invest your time, attention, and efforts in your most important priorities**. When I work with business leaders, I often do this exercise with them, which I call The 50 Choices Dilemma. This dramatically clarifies how they think about and make decisions. I'll say, "You have 50 things to do today. I'm going to give you two choices. You can handle priorities 1, 2, and 3 but never touch the other 47, or you can handle priorities 4 to 50 and never touch 1, 2, and 3. What is your choice?"

When they hear these options, many people are drawn to the idea of clearing off 47 things from their to-do list. However, they also know that is a very poor choice, and everybody knows the smart choice is handling priorities 1, 2, and 3. **Choosing priorities 1, 2, and 3 is common sense – but it is *not* common practice**. Not for salespeople, not for clients, and unfortunately, not for very many.

If you want to prove yourself to be an extraordinarily valuable partner from the very first moment you talk to a client, then you need to help them get clear about what is most valuable, important, and has the highest impact result for their company. That's worth a whole lot more for both of you to go after. Remember the $8 million, three-years-in-the-making disaster? The client didn't understand what was most important to them, and the service provider did what they were asked. What resulted was an enormous amount of wasted time, energy, and resources. And it was all because of poorly understood priorities. The service provider was so focused on delivering what the client had asked for that they didn't do what was most important. They failed to clarify whether what they were being asked for was really what was most needed and valuable.

THE NEW 80/20 RULE

Vilfredo Pareto was an Italian economist who, in 1906, postulated what we now know as the 80/20 rule. He was studying land ownership in Italy, and he found that 80 percent of the land was owned by 20 percent of the people. But what clinched the rule for him was when he discovered that 80 percent of the peas in his garden came from 20 percent of the pods. Thus was born the 80/20 rule, or Pareto's law, which states that roughly 80 percent of effects come from 20 percent of sources.

My 80/20 rule was born by observing what the best of the best do and what everybody else does. Here is **my New 80/20 Rule: 80 percent of success Is common sense – but less than 20 percent of the people are using it**. Focusing on your top priorities is obviously common sense. For a variety of reasons, including the fact that it can take some time and thoughtful dialogue to know what those top priorities are, this is not common enough practice in business today. If you really want to provide the ultimate value

The New 80/20 Rule continued

to your clients – the kind that is not only going to win you business but will also win you more business over a longer period of time – then **your job is to help your clients turn common sense into common practice to produce massively uncommon results**.

Now that you have a picture forming of why a serious gap exists between how sales is practiced today and what clients really need and want, let's talk about a better approach. In the next chapter, you will learn about how **instead of selling clients what you have, you can become an Indispensable Partner in their success**. And that approach works massively better for you and your client in producing exceptionally valuable results.

CHAPTER THREE

A NEW PARADIGM – BECOMING THE INDISPENSABLE PARTNER IN YOUR CLIENTS' SUCCESS

"The difficulty lies not so much in developing new ideas as in escaping from old ones."

—JOHN MAYNARD KEYNES

What is being proposed in this book is a fundamental and radical shift in the sales relationship and how to build it for massive success. In the old, classic sales relationship, the one most people are practicing today, the salesperson comes in with his bag of offerings, and it is his job to figure out which one of those offerings fits the client's situation. Then he has to persuade the client that his "well-considered" solution will ease the client's pain and solve the problem that has been put on the table.

The fundamental premise is that the salesperson's focus is on finding a way to get the clients to see that what he has is what the client needs. He is focused on finding gaps in the client's processes or organization that he can fill. This is classic thinking for most salespeople today – even good and reasonably success-ful ones. This is the "puzzle piece" approach to sales that I talked about previously, and especially in high-level professional services sales, it is never as clean and simple as putting one of your pieces into the client's puzzle. Success requires understanding, clarity, flexibility, adaptability, and a deep understanding of the results that would ultimately be most valuable and lead to real success.

Here is the revolutionary idea this book proposes: **Your job as a salesperson, first and foremost, is to make sure that your client is focused on and understands what is really most important and valuable for themselves and their organization. You are a facilitator of what is most important for that client, helping him focus on, define, and understand what really matters most and is most critical for the success of his organization.**

This is a fundamentally different idea about how the sales process needs to work. It literally flips the entire game on its head. It is not about you trying to figure out what the clients needs so you can see how to get what you have into their hands. **It is about building the kind of trust, openness, respect, and communication that leads to a high-trust relationship, one where the client gets real value from the way you facilitate and help them build a depth of clarity and understanding.** Your focus is on making sure that what the client is asking for is really going to help them and their company achieve significant and powerful results. **Your ability to facilitate this kind of clarity – for them – is the key to being valued not for what you have to sell but for who you can be as a powerful partner in their success.** This kind of relationship raises you above your competition and the solutions they are pushing.

You are helping the client to define the most significant solutions they really need, which most times is not what they originally asked for. **When you help clients focus on what would really serve them best, you assume a position of trust that is beyond offering mere solutions.** With this approach, you are in a position to demonstrate value from your very first conversation. That conversation is all about them and getting to what is most important – and not in the least about you and what you are selling. This is your powerful switch of focus and intention.

Axiom #1 of The Ultimate Sales Revolution:
The fastest way to prove how valuable you are is to deliver value from the very first conversation – which has nothing to do with what you have to sell.

BECOMING AN INDISPENSABLE PARTNER

Becoming an indispensable partner in your clients' success is the most effective approach to achieving long-term success for both the client and the salesperson. What is needed is not for you, as the salesperson, to tell the client your story. It requires something very different than for you to dump pages of specifications on a client that they will barely understand. What it really requires is for you to facilitate clarity and understanding about their top priorities, even though it's likely that they are not crystal clear about them themself. By helping them be successful in their current situation, in their department, and on behalf of their entire company, you both establish clear value for them, *and* you learn about what really matters to them.

That is the critical outcome that salespeople today need to be focused on. But it is also one that far too few people understand. Your demonstration that you can help a client and their company become successful has the highest level of impact and proves that you are worth working with. If you come in and provide the client excellent approaches that solve their current issue or satisfies their

INDISPENSABLE PARTNER – A DEFINITION

This is the highest level of professional success: becoming an Indispensable Partner in your clients' success. Helping them get clear about what matters most, focusing on their highest-impact results, and being successful at delivering an exceptional level of value, positions you as their Indispensable Partner. **You are seen as someone who is invaluable in helping a client become clearer, make better decisions, and maintain focus on what is most important, while providing the superior services and products that deliver these outstanding results.** This is where high value technical competence and high impact relational skills come together to produce the most remarkable results.

Remember that your greatest differentiation and ability to position yourself above your competition starts with outstanding relational skills – the way you dramatically demonstrate real and meaningful value before they even buy anything.

boss who is pushing them, you might be able to get a deal. But what happens when that deal does not deliver what the client and his company really needed most? What happens is that your perceived value, reputation, and standing as a worthwhile partner are seriously diminished. It will be extremely difficult, if not impossible, to generate more business with that client. And that is the opposite of what you want.

Instead, **to succeed at the highest levels in today's world, what you must do is become an Indispensable Partner in the success of your client**. What that means is that you are consistently so valuable to them that they see you as a fabulous partner in achieving their short- and long-term success. As a result, they bring you in early on planning, instead of just handing you the specifications that they think they need. They consult with you and seek your insight when they have questions, instead of just trying to figure things out for themselves. They see you as somebody who provides so much value in so many ways that in their mind, you become an indispensable part of achieving their success. **Not your success but *their* success.** Of course, helping them achieve meaningful and significant success is the best way to guarantee your ultimate success.

INDISPENSABLE PARTNER GRID

The Indispensable Partner Paradigm

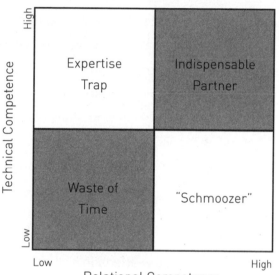

©2015 Optimize International

Becoming an Indispensable Partner requires combining high technical expertise with the highest level of relational expertise to produce meaningful impact, value, and results for your clients.

You can see on the grid that one axis is technical skills. That could mean your technical skills as a financial advisor, engineer, I.T. professional, doctor, lawyer, accountant, consultant, or whatever professional expertise you offer clients. The other axis is relational skills. That means your ability to communicate and to build value-based relationships where the clients recognize they can really trust you to help them reach their highest level of impact, value, and success.

How effective you are depends on where you stand on both axes. If you have low relational skills and low technical skills, then you're useless in all meaningful ways. If you have high technical skill and low relational skills, you fall into what I call the "expertise trap." Most people, especially the people I work with regularly, have developed superior levels of technical expertise. Someone with that level of technical skills often understands the issues and solutions before their client has even talked through all of their symptoms and issues. They are also right most of the time when it comes to matters that fall within their area of expertise.

This is the kind of salesperson who often walks in, gives the client the right answer, and then is surprised and disappointed to find that the client doesn't appreciate nor value it. They are appalled that their brilliant – and usually correct – diagnosis and solution is not respected or accepted. When ultimately proven right, they are likely to complain with frustration: "I told them the right answer, but they didn't pay attention."

Axiom #2 of The Ultimate Sales Revolution:
Being right is insufficient for being effective.

Every time I share this all-too-true axiom, laughter erupts when I say: "Anyone who is married knows what I'm talking about." Being right is not enough in any important relationship, particularly in today's environment. You may be an expert and understand your products and services brilliantly, but then why is it that people don't care when you give them the answers you know they need?

There are two critical perspectives to understand to excel at the relational side of sales today. The first is that **your answer is only valued when the client understands and appreciates the importance of the issues you are addressing with your solution and services.** Given that clients often have their heads down and are paying attention only to the next steps or actions they hope will make a difference, your facilitating clarity about the meaningful impact, value, and results they really need shifts their perspective on what their real issues and opportunities are.

This shift of perspective serves to help clients appreciate the bigger situation, the larger opportunity, and the greater value that they can realize. The very act of helping them shift their focus to a higher level of results opens up their thinking and willingness to consider new ideas, approaches, and ways of dealing with the issues they are facing.

This shift is akin to driving down the highway in the usual half-attentive state. Suddenly a situation comes up forcing you to be fully aware of your surroundings and reconsider your driving choices more consciously – perhaps to avoid an accident or potential danger in the road. **Creating this state of alertness to the greater situation, rather than having your client continue driving "on automatic," is important in every significant buying encounter**. Otherwise, as we have seen, 80 to 90 percent of the time their "automatic" is going to miss the most valuable opportunities and solutions.

The second critical perspective to understand is this: **Most of the time people cannot competently judge your level of technical expertise and especially as compared to your top competitors.**

How do I understand the technical knowledge and capability that my attorney has? How do I know if he's better than the big-name lawyers next door? How do I technically judge if my financial advisor is better than my last one or the one in the office upstairs? Trial and error? As Henry Ford said, "The school of experience is the best one there is. Unfortunately by the time you graduate, you're too old, too tired, or too poor to do anything about it."

The point is that when we're talking about top technical services providers and salespeople, the client can't tell the difference between you and your competitors when it comes to your technical competence and expertise. The client is not usually technically proficient enough to judge the difference between the top choices, which is why he needs to bring in a top professional to help him. So figuring out who is the most technically competent is not how he is going to decide whom to hire.

The critical deciding factor for a client is who he trusts most and believes is most likely to take care of him, his company, and his clients in an area where he frankly cannot tell how technically and professionally competent his options are. He needs to trust, respect, and feel a connection with the person he will hire. What better way to demonstrate that you are the best one to help him generate the most meaningful results than by helping him get clear about and focused on what really matters and would generate the greatest impact and value? He hires the person he trusts the most to take care of him in the best possible way, even though he doesn't know exactly what that will take.

When the client lacks trust and the conviction that he's got somebody he can really rely on to take care of his best interests, he falls back on spelling out in massive detail what he thinks he wants. Of course, most of these details, actions, and activities are not what would be most important. They can also mire a supplier in a cycle of details that will not deliver what would be most valuable. **The more trust you have with a client, the more the two of you can elevate your focus to valuable outcomes. The less trust you have, the more the focus will be on the details, minutia, and specifications of the project.**

People with high relational skills and low technical skills fall into the schmoozer category. This is the quadrant too many traditional salespeople fall into. These are the people who try to talk their way into business, acting like a friend or buddy who is going to take care of you. What every savvy professional and client knows is that once the deal is done, likely so is the attention they are getting. Schmoozers give professional sales a bad name because of all their talking, pushiness, manipulation, and ability to avoid dealing with the critical criteria required for the success of their clients – and sometimes even their own companies.

The final quadrant is where you find the professionals with both high technical skills and high relational skills. These are the most successful sales professionals, whom we call the Indispensable Partners in their clients' – and their own company's – success. **This is the highest level of professional relationship, the one where your client respects, recognizes, and rewards you commensurate with your being an Indispensable Partner in their success.**

How do you get there? You can get there very quickly. You don't have to spend a lot of time or go through a lot of activities to prove yourself to be an Indispensable Partner. Achieving this standing with clients starts with the way you treat people, communicate with them, and build a relationship with them, especially where you help them get clear about what is most important to them.

The focus is on connecting them to what is most important to their business, not on figuring out how to get your products or services into their hands. In fact, it is not about you at all! The conversation of a top-notch salesperson is focused entirely on the client and on facilitating their understanding and commitment to what is most important, meaningful, and valuable to them.

TRANSACTIONAL VS. HIGH-VALUE RELATIONSHIPS

The kind of "here is how I can help you" or "here is my bag of offerings" relationship that is so common today is based upon purely transactional relationships. Salespeople who are building only transactional relationships come at sales from the perspective of, "I don't know you well. I don't know what you need. I don't know what your company's priorities are. But I know you're buying services, and I've got what you need. So, let me show you why we're better than anybody else. Let me show you all the clients I've dealt with who are like you, and let me spec your requirements so we can give you a competitive bid." In the previous chapters, we learned about the reasons why that kind of approach would fail – especially when competing against a competent Ultimate Sales Revolution practitioner.

Despite the examples of failure that I've described, this approach will sound pretty familiar to most people because it is so common. It is the kind of relationship we encounter too often in business and why most people don't want to talk to salespeople who operate like this. Sales, as it is commonly practiced today, is too much about the salesperson banging on the door, talking too much about themselves, and providing too little value to the client. Why would a client care about that?

Here is the problem: If you're a transactional salesperson, you might win business, but you're probably going to have to win it on the basis of price. That's going to happen for three reasons: 1) You haven't elevated your standing with the client by facilitating their clarity about the high-impact results that would be most valuable to them, 2) You have not educated the client about what differentiates you from your competition in delivering optimal value to him, and 3) The client probably can't tell whether you have any technical superiority or difference from your competitors.

High-value relationships, by contrast, are not based on transactions and price. In fact, the third axiom of The Ultimate Sales Revolution is critical to understand if you are aiming to create those differentiating, high-impact, trusting relationships:

Axiom #3 of The Ultimate Sales Revolution:
Price is never an issue – unless the value isn't clear.

The primary focus of the best and most successful relationships is on facilitating the highest and best-possible outcomes and results with the client and for the overall success of the client's business. I explain the differences between the two kinds of relationships on the next page. In this kind of relationship, you seek to influence the client at their highest possible level of impact. And by affecting them on the highest possible level – including by contributing to their company's most important outcomes – you maximize the impact, value, and results you deliver. By clearly maximizing value to the client and their company, you create a high likelihood of being chosen as the one they want. Your demonstration of value – before you have been hired or even charged them anything – also makes price a secondary concern relative to all of the value you can provide. That is the key to optimizing your revenues and profitability, both short and long term.

Put it this way: I can either fulfill your requests and help you be successful with these for this quarter or this year (a transactional approach), or I can help you be a major contributor to your company's most critical successes (the Indispensable Partner, high-value approach). Which are you and your clients going to choose more often – and pay more for?

TRANSACTIONAL RELATIONSHIP	HIGH-VALUE RELATIONSHIP
The primary focus is on the task or transaction to be completed.	The primary focus is on the overall success of the relationship and the client's business.
» The focus is on each individual interaction and what we think we have to do to make the transaction happen successfully.	» The focus is on being a partner in accelerating and expanding the success of the client and their company which takes precedence over any individual transaction or project.
» The greatest attention is paid to what is being worked on, what we are doing, and how we are being treated and evaluated within this transaction.	» Special arrangements or concessions may be made on an individual project when it advances the overall success of the partnership.
» The focus is on solving the client's current strategic or tactical problems.	» High-value relationships focus on helping the client fulfill their missions and goals.
» Transactional relationships suffer from competitive and pricing pressures and a client mindset that "you are only as good as your last deliverable."	» In high-value relationships, additional new business opportunities become more available as you build trust and respect.

You'll discover the principles and practices for building this kind of high value, Indispensable Partner success in the rest of this book. One concern that many people have raised about this Indispensable Partner idea is whether it will take a long time to build this kind of relationship with a client and to sort out what is most important to them. Let me answer that concern as simply and clearly as I can – it does not. In fact, over the long run, it takes much less time to produce significantly more and better results.

In your first conversation with a client, you might need an extra 30 or 60 minutes. However, approaching sales in this way will save weeks, if not months, by avoiding mistakes, miscommunications, misalignments, and issues down the road. It will also keep you focused on the top priorities so you aren't wasting time doing low-value or unimportant work. People who think it is too difficult or time-consuming to develop this sort of relationship with a client are simply not doing it in an effective way. The second half of this book shows you exactly what you need to do to optimize your success and the impact, value, and results of your clients.

THE DIFFERENCE SEVEN MINUTES CAN MAKE

Very early in my career, I ran a toy company, and we created stickers as a major product. We were selling a three-cent product, and today my clients focus on deals worth $300,000 to $30 million. What is noteworthy is that the fundamentals for success are really the same.

One day I called up Target, the number-two retailer at the time, because through my research I had learned that they were about to put in a major addition to their stationery department. Getting the buyer on the phone, I asked, "Are you working on putting together a highly successful sticker program for your stores? How open are you to some new and different approaches that will make you even more successful in this category?"

I didn't say, "I have something for you. I've got the best product. You should talk to me." No, the question I led with was all about them; it was not about me.

Still, the buyer told me: "Thank you, but I think we are almost totally set, and we really don't need any more help." I was about to be shut out of the number-two retailer, when I said to her, "Would you be willing to invest seven minutes to examine how this could help your program be even better and more successful?" I was in Boston, and this buyer's office was in Minneapolis, so I made this offer: "If you are open to seeing some additional ways to be even more successful and profitable with your program, and you will schedule seven minutes to check this out, I will fly to Minneapolis to meet you. If what you are seeing is not valuable to you and your program, I will leave your office after seven minutes."

What would anyone say to that? She said, "If you're willing to come out for seven minutes, I'll see you."

When she welcomed me into her office a few days later, I put a watch down with a seven-minute timer on it and started talking. But what would be the best things you could possibly say to make an impact in seven minutes? The answer is not to say much at all. Instead, I started asking her questions, all focused on her, her program, and her key objectives.

"What are the most important results you're committed to achieving with this program?"

She answered that question.

"How confidant are you – on a zero to 100 percent scale – that you have exactly what you need to be successful?"

She said, "Seventy-five or eighty percent."

"Would you be open to raising that level of confidence and success?"

"Yes, of course I would."

"Are you open to considering some changes and suggestions about what would make your program even more successful?"

"Yes, of course I am."

Seven minutes was almost up. I picked up my watch and said, "My seven minutes is up," and I stood up to leave. She told me to sit down, and an hour later, I walked out with one of the largest orders my company had ever won.

The whole approach was all about her and increasing her success. It had nothing to do with me or my products – except where I could serve her ultimate, most important outcomes. That is the difference here: **It is all about the client, their needs, their most important outcomes, and their success**. Until we understand that, and the client perceives that is our focus and intention, it is premature and even destructive to start talking about what it is we have, what we do, and why we're their best choice. In fact, **you turn people off by discussing your products and services when they aren't confident that you understand their needs. This is the difference between simply selling something and demonstrating value in such a way that the client starts to see you as a valuable partner.** This is key to building your foundation with clients as an Indispensable Partner in their success.

THE FACILITATOR ROLE

Regardless of what your position is, whether you call yourself a salesperson, manager, or a leader, if you work with other people **your most fundamental job and most powerful platform for success is to be a facilitator of what is most important to**

your clients. That means remembering the lessons of the Three Sources of Miscommunication, including understanding that 80 to 90 percent of the time your clients are not clearly focused on or communicating what is most important to them. But when they don't know or are not clearly focused on this, it is one of your greatest opportunities to demonstrate how much value you can deliver.

You do this by facilitating clarity about what is most important – which is what the second part of this book will teach you how to do. You will learn, step-by-step, how human communication – done well – can be leveraged into a high-quality relationship that demonstrates and creates value. Remember, **the creation of value is the strongest and most universal way to build great relationships**. Through that process of communicating and building a high quality relationship, you can differentiate yourself massively from a typical salesperson – I don't care how good they are – in terms of the value you can deliver. **Value creation and delivery is the defining factor for massive success, and that starts happening with your very first conversation**. That is the Ultimate Sales Revolution in action!

We will cover exactly what you need to do in Part II of this book, but first, it is critical to understand that you will be performing a fundamentally different role in your relationship with your clients. If you don't understand this and shift your perspective, oftentimes people just revert back to "Let me tell you what I can do for you" – the classic salesperson you most certainly don't want to be.

As an Indispensable Partner in your client's success, it is your role and responsibility to make it easy for them to:

☐ Find

☐ Uncover

☐ Recognize

☐ Get clear about what is most valuable to them.

Again, it is essential that this becomes your mindset in every encounter as you demonstrate the value you can bring them – from your very first conversation.

THE BENEFITS OF BEING AN INDISPENSABLE PARTNER IN THEIR SUCCESS

As I said from the beginning, this common-sense, yet radical, approach to sales success leads to massively better results. Here is what you can expect to get out of becoming an Indispensable Partner:

1. **You are going to get paid for your value**, not for the amount of activity, time, or effort you expend on behalf of your client. That's important, because if you are getting paid for activity, time, or effort, you are going to be priced like a commodity. Commodities are always about being sold at the lowest price possible. **Value is negotiated not on the basis of price but on the basis of impact, results, and ability to move the client's business forward.**

2. The **relationship is far more sustainable** and transcends merely moving from one transaction to the next. Transactional relationships can actually span 20 years or more. However, you know it is a transactional

relationship when you get dropped, regardless of how long you have worked with a client, because another vendor comes in with a lower price. That demonstrates you were a convenient, price-driven vendor, who didn't have a value-based partnership or relationship.

Another way to tell you are in a transactional relationship is when there is a big screw-up – and screw-ups happen in relationships, especially when it comes to complex projects and services. When that happens, your client's response in a transactional relationship is: "*You* screwed up. *You* need to fix this, or I'm getting somebody else."

When you have a high-value partnership, the response is: "*We* have a problem *we* need to solve." As a real, trusted, and high value partner, it becomes *our* problem, not *your* problem, or *you* screwed up.

Transactional relationships are looked at from the point of view of pricing and convenience, where you are only as good as your last deal. That makes them hard to sustain – certainly on a profitable basis. High value, Indispensable Partner relationships are treasured, trusted, and respected. The desire for mutual best interests comes from the client's side as well as yours. Issues are not dumped in your lap but are approached as they would be in any great relationship – looking for a great mutual solution, rather than blame.

3. Another benefit of this approach is that **you're going to know earlier whether or not someone is going to be a good client**. You're going to know whether a potential client is the type of person who can think in a meaningful way, on a deep level about their priorities, and is open to

support in moving forward on what is most important to them. Another one of my observations is that **the best clients are always the ones who are most committed to getting better.** The ones who are obstructionists, difficult, and basically naysayers are: a) typically low-level thinkers; b) too easily fixated on small issues. If you can't get someone focused on what is most important, then you're not going to be very successful in becoming an Indispensable Partner in their success because they'll get stuck in transactional negotiations; and c) not going to be highly successful over the long term.

Knowing early who is going to be a tough, hard, or bad client can save you weeks, if not months, if not years, of frustration, difficulty, and finally failure. By putting in just a few extra minutes in the beginning, you can discover if someone is open to focusing on what is most important and open to a partnership for accelerating and expanding their success – or not.

Remember, my first big Fortune 500 client was won after just one hour and five minutes with a key decision maker. He had already spent six days with my competitor, who had not shown enough understanding of what really mattered to the client in that time to win the trust, respect, and confidence that he could be successful in helping them with their real business issues. In 65 minutes of mostly asking the appropriate questions, getting the client focused on what was really most important – and getting them away from what they had prematurely defined as their solution – the trust, respect, and confidence was built to win the business at four times the investment the guy who had six days with them had proposed. This is just one common sense demonstration that in the long run, the Ultimate Sales Revolution approach is not just a more effective and efficient way to do business, it is a much more profitable and successful way as well.

EQUATIONS FOR SUCCESS

When you are working as an Indispensable Partner in your client's success, with a focus on maximizing the impact, value, and results they can achieve, the equation for success becomes much more interesting and compelling than just typical specifications and price. You have the opportunity – and responsibility – to build an equation beyond the mere details of your products and services. The power of this approach is in making clear how your clients, their business, their company, and their clients are going to achieve what would be most valuable to them.

This is especially true when they are part of the 80 to 90 percent of clients who ask for a solution that is nowhere near as meaningful, valuable, or powerful as it could be. **Your facilitation literally changes the equation for success and separates you from all of your competition who are solving the problem they were given.**

As an example, one of my clients was a major print broker whose largest client accounted for 15 percent of their business. Their client, a giant financial institution, got a new CFO, who naturally said, "I want to lower our costs." So, he put their long-standing contract out to bid in the market.

Now, this print broker used the best, highest-quality, most reliable resources possible and consolidated everything. They were competitive but never meant to be the lowest price. Naturally, everybody was in a panic when this CFO said he wanted the lowest price.

This is a great example of a client who didn't fully think through what was most important. What the print broker did for the client was print materials explaining the company's financial products, which they would send to all their distributors, partners, and salespeople, which numbered in the thousands. Instead of lowering their prices to match the other bids, I got my client to build an equation for real success for their client.

They calculated their on-time delivery rate, which was an outstanding 99.98 percent over the prior few years. They calculated their accuracy rate, meaning how often they got very detailed and legally significant materials flawless – a highly meaningful, value-added, and critical step. That, too, was nearly 100 percent. Then they put together a fuller picture of what they offered the client beyond just what the price of printed materials was going to be. They went back to the CFO and said, "Here is what a 1 percent error from your partner represents to you. It would mean you've got as many as 40 of your top people unable to use your materials or sell your product. And here is what that would mean over the course of a year when you're shipping as many as 30 sets of materials annually. Now you've got as many as 1,200 failures to deliver on a key product initiative, and here is what that could be worth in terms of average sales."

When the new CFO started to look at these things, the fact that my client was 20 percent more than the lowest bid made real economic and business sense. My client won the business because the ultimate equation for success consisted of far more than the mere cost of the product. Failing to deliver accurate materials on time produced a dramatic impediment to the ultimate success of this financial institution that went far beyond the differential in price. In fact, the value of the reliability and accuracy they provided was so significant that the premium their client paid to get it was worth many times the price differential. It had massive, quantifiable value to their client's ultimate success.

Of course my client won the business and the respect and appreciation of their client's CFO for opening his eyes to what was needed for his company's ultimate success. This built a stronger, more-trusting relationship between their companies that lasted many more years. That is the power of a well-defined equation for success.

Again, this is a case of **helping the client succeed at what they need most, rather than just giving them what they ask for**. Of course they want a lower price. But what they really want is to increase the critical success factors in their business. They want to ensure their reputation. They want to make sure their people have the tools they need to support the initiatives necessary for generating continued growth and success. And yes, of course they want lower prices, but smart clients and salespeople prioritize that in the context of the overall value proposition for business success. My client was shocked – and elated – when they won the business. I wasn't shocked at all; this is how you win important clients and their business.

Who would you rather buy from? The company who is going to cut his price by a fraction of a penny to save you some money or the company who is going to help you be far more successful at ensuring your business grows and thrives in all the most important ways and, by the way, will give you a reasonable price for that too.

Because I understood my client, I could put together what I call their equation for success. What is the equation for success? If it is only about the price, then you are being too shallow and too ignorant of what your client is trying to achieve. **Being an Indispensable Partner is about delivering the greatest impact, value, and results for your client**. And that holds true even when the guy is telling you that price is what he cares about most.

The best and most successful salespeople must be tuned to deliver what is most important, not what a client is fixated on, especially when that is not what matters most.

Done well, selling is one of the most exhilarating professional relationships we can have. Too few people think like that – even people who love to sell. When you really understand what is critical to a successful relationship, you have enormous power to enhance the entire process. It is not about you trying to fit into someone else's world. That is the old way of thinking.

Instead, **the most powerful and valuable relationships are the ones where someone gets an exceptional amount of value from being in a relationship with you.** When you are delivering an exceptional amount of value in that relationship, it opens up massive opportunities for you to receive exceptional value as well.

That is the opportunity this book holds for you. It teaches you how to deliver massive amounts of value to your clients and get massive value in return. Let's continue by shedding some of the old ways of practicing sales in the next chapter: The Sales Exorcism.

CHAPTER FOUR

THE SALES EXORCISM

"Perfection of means and confusion of ends
seem to characterize our age."

—ALBERT EINSTEIN

As we all know, salespeople are not highly regarded, respected, and appreciated by many people. This is a cultural artifact that is rooted in a poor understanding of how to build value, as well as the poor relationship practices of many salespeople. It has evolved to become a visceral response when most people meet a salesperson.

What are your first thoughts about a salesperson and selling when one walks up to you in a store?

I've done this exercise with all sorts of people and groups around the world, and the typical responses are neither pretty nor positive. The most common first responses are:

1. Coercion

2. Manipulation

3. Wants me to buy something

4. Wants to force me to buy something

5. Talks too much

81

6. Is self-interested, and mostly focused on what they want

7. Doesn't really know what I need or want

8. Doesn't really care about what I need or want

9. Feigns interest but doesn't really care about me

10. Wants the sale more than anything

11. Will say anything to get the sale

12. Willing to lie to get what he wants

13. Won't tell me the whole story

14. Can be deceptive

15. Interested in getting what he wants far more than me getting what I want

These are typically the first 15 responses and how most people think about sales and salespeople. Many clients are checking you out when you talk with them to see if you are "one of those." If you're a salesperson, you have to ask yourself if you're provoking any of these reactions in the people you are selling to. If this is what people are thinking when you show up, then you have a huge barrier to get over before they want to deal with you. If you inspire any of these reactions, you're going to have difficulty. If you inspire three or more of them, you are prone to far more failure than you should have.

If when people talk to you they're thinking about manipulation, coercion, feeling forced, and so on, those are indicators that you have bad communication and a very limited relationship with your client.

This is the exorcism that needs to take place about sales – recognizing that the cultural, and even our own personal thoughts, often tend toward these negative, demeaning, disrespectful, and disreputable thoughts about the sales process. To prepare you for getting over this old and unproductive thinking requires starting with what I call the "sales exorcism." This is about abandoning the old manipulative ways to make room for real success.

As you consider the list of 15 of the most common – and unfortunately negative – responses people have to sales and salespeople, evaluate whether any of your clients would say any of these about you. Consider whether you say any of these about you. For each negative that you honestly could say applies to your influence or sales approach, write out what you would prefer to be known for instead.

The true "exorcism" of these negative and nasty approaches comes when you dedicate yourself to conducting your communication and relationships consistent with becoming an Indispensable Partner. When neither you nor any of your clients would pin any of those negatives above on your influence, persuasion, or sales approaches, you have successfully exorcised the outdated and less effective sales techniques.

With that exorcism comes the openness to the principles and skills of the Ultimate Sales Revolution. These are built to create entirely different responses, the kind people have identified as the most desirable traits of their ideal salesperson:

1. Listens well

2. Is honest and trustworthy

3. Has excellent communication skills

4. Helps me get clear about what I really need

5. Focuses on what is really important

6. Supports me in communicating with my boss or other decision makers

7. Takes responsibility and keeps his promises

8. Helps me be more successful

9. Always has my best interests in mind

10. Provides more value than I even expected

These are essential for building the kind of relationship you want to have. Here is the critical, four-step sequence for how human dynamics creates that kind of result:

1. Quality of communication, which develops the

2. Quality of relationship, which allows for the

3. Demonstration of value, which builds to

4. Being an Indispensable Partner in their success.

Alternatively, you might take clients for a round of golf or out to dinner or a ballgame, which is how salespeople try to influence relationships that are not substantive. Really that is just another, more subtle, form of manipulation. Your client may take you up on the round of golf, but they see it for what it is.

One of my clients had an outside auditing firm partner who invited my client's controller to many conferences around the world. In return, the controller was giving the outside auditing firm many millions of dollars a year in business. When the controller left, that auditing firm had to fight for the same business because that form of manipulation wasn't as effective with the new decision maker.

Suppose, instead, the focus was on what would be valuable to you, as a client. Instead of primarily giving you gifts and taking you places, we make sure that together we are driving toward what is ultimately most important to you and your organization. I ensure that what we're doing is actually serving and supporting your and your organization's top priorities – what you really need most. In this case, you're not just getting "perks" so you feel like you owe me something. You're getting to see that when we work together you're going to be clearer, more focused, and have greater success and impact.

Which person do you want to buy from – the charming one who gives you gifts or the one who supports you in producing the greatest impact, value, and results on what is really important to you? Not just what you're asking for but what is *really* meaningful to you and your organization.

This is being an Indispensable Partner, and to make this switch from the old ways of selling is going to require the fundamental mindset shift we have been talking about.

TWO KEYS TO IMPROVING RESULTS

Even if you understand the need to be an Indispensable Partner conceptually, it can be difficult not to fall back into old habits. Too many salespeople have habitually taken a transactional approach, rather than a high value, Indispensable Partner approach to selling.

If you want to get better results, there are two changes that will do it. Change your actions, or change your mindset. You're going to have to do both. However, the problem with just changing your actions is that people often have trouble getting away from their old ways. They fall back on old habits, especially when they're stressed or pressured. And here is another of my favorite truths.

Axiom #4 of The Ultimate Sales Revolution:
The greatest impediment to change is habits.

Since habits are the biggest impediment to making a change, especially big ones, you need to start with mindset. Change the way you think about sales and your client relationships, and change in your actions will follow.

CHANGE YOUR SALES LANGUAGE

If you look at the sales process as currently practiced, it is oriented around language like: *I need to get an appointment with you.* Or, *I want to tell you about our latest offerings.* Or, *Let me show you what I've got and why we're the best choice.*

When most people think about practicing sales today, they think about their need to *convince* the other person. In order to do that, they have to do things like *probe* their client and *dig deeper* into what the client is telling them. And then they need to *close the sale*. These are the vernacular of the typical old-fashioned sales process and what the old way of thinking looks like.

The problem with this way of doing business is that we know by now that it is way too much about me and what I'm going to do to you as my client. You can see it in the very language that is used. The language centers on *I, me*, and *we*. Not on *you*, the client.

Being an Indispensable Partner, much like a great marriage or friendship, means I provide value for you based on what you need most. That starts by working to understand what you really need and would value most. Suppose you tell me, "I need 70 million dollars' worth of desktop computers." That is not what you really need. Those computers are the means by which you will achieve some outcome. An Indispensable Partner gets you clear about and committed to what the high-value result of those computers will be. **The value of a meaningful result is often worth multiples of any process that will get you to that result.**

Successful sales is about ensuring that you, as the client, are focused on what is most important and most valuable for you, your department, your organization, and your clients. The best sales-people ensure that your priorities are clear and meaningful and that what you want to do is consistent with what would produce the greatest impact, value, and results for you. Great salespeople make sure that you're making the best decisions on your own behalf. Effective human dynamics requires that the language you use is consistent with and supports that idea. **The language you choose must tell your listener that you care about them and what is most important to them.**

One of the things I tell people to do when they're looking to become Indispensable Partners is to, as much as possible, stop using "I," "me," and "we" in your conversation. Most people ask: "Can I make an appointment with you?" or "Do you have some time to tell me about what you are looking for?" or "Could you tell me more about that?" Why are you the subject of your communications with your client?

◊ **Axiom #5 of The Ultimate Sales Revolution:**
To shift your mindset to becoming an Indispensable Partner, to the degree possible eliminate I, me, and we from your conversation.

Instead, you could say: "You're looking to purchase some servers. Would it be valuable to you to discuss options that can improve the speed and service and create the most effective implementation?"

That's a different question than, "Can I schedule some time to talk about the servers you want to buy?"

If, as a salesperson, you start saying, "I'd like to discuss that with you," you have to ask yourself, why should this person care what you want? They're busy and have their own pressures. However, "Would you be interested in seeing better ways to address the most critical issues in your business?" is the kind of language that opens up a different conversation – and perspective. Recognize that people who say no to a question like that are not going to be good clients or thoughtful people. You may still give them a second chance, but if somebody is not interested in looking at better ways to address their most critical issues, then that person is a fool. It is much better to know that as early as possible.

THE LANGUAGE OF SELLING: ME VS. YOU

To understand the difference between Me (old way of selling) vs. You (Indispensable Partner orientation) ways of speaking, consider the different lines of dialogues from a variety of sales professions. Note that the most effective way to be "you focused" is to ask questions that are valuable to them, rather than make statements about yourself.

INVESTMENT ADVISOR

"Me" Orientation: "I would like to review your portfolio with you."

"You" Orientation: "How confident are you that your portfolio is exactly where you want it to be?"

"Me" Orientation: "I would love to make some suggestions about your financial plan."

"You" Orientation: "Would it be of significant value to examine whether your financial plan is meeting your most important objectives?"

IT PROFESSIONAL

"Me" Orientation: "I'd like to show you how you can improve your overall operating efficiency."

"You" Orientation: "How valuable would it be to you to review how to upgrade your operational effectiveness?"

"Me" Orientation: "I can show you how to get greater productivity at a lower cost."

"You" Orientation: "How open are you to considering how to lower your costs while increasing your productivity?"

PHARMACEUTICAL REP

"Me" Orientation: "I'd like to discuss our new drug that just came out."

"You" Orientation: "Would it be valuable to discuss a potential new solution for your most critically needy patients that could address one of their big challenges?"

"Me" Orientation: "I'd like to talk to you about some ways to improve patient outcomes."

"You" Orientation: "Would you be willing to invest three minutes to ensure you have safer, faster, more effective protocols for taking care of your patients?"

THE POWER OF COMMUNICATION

In my first job as a salesperson, I had a big opportunity with a major client. My wife, who worked with me at the time, went with me. I was selling posters and art prints, and this client was a big chain, so it represented a great opportunity. We walked out with an order. Then my wife turned to me and said, "Do you know how many times you said 'fantastic' during that meeting?" I said, "I don't know. Six or seven?" She said, "I stopped counting after 75." Apparently, I kept saying things like: "This product is fantastic.

This one is so fantastic, it's a best selling... Now, this one is *really* fantastic."

Deeply embarrassed, I resolved then and there that I would learn how to communicate effectively and certainly expand my vocabulary. I recognized that I was repeating myself and sounding fake but also that I was talking about what I had and my opinions about it. Looking back, it was all about my point of view, instead of being about the client and their perspective. Compare that to my opening question in the "Would you invest seven minutes" story told in the last chapter: "How open are you to some new and different approaches that will make you much more successful in this category?"

This is about much more than just the language. The language used represents a fundamental shift in perspective. The approaches in these two stories represent very different mindsets. Virtually every salesperson I've ever talked to has their personal agenda burning a hole in their back pocket, like I did early in my career. What happens is their agenda is so present, it is like a vibrating phone in their pocket all the time. So when they're talking to clients, they might be trying to be client focused, but what they're really doing is trying to figure out, "How do I get my puzzle piece into his puzzle, so that he sees the fit?"

Your primary agenda should be clarifying your client's most important and fundamental results. That's how you become an Indispensable Partner. Good communication is key to that, and you'll start the process there in the next section. Here are some key communication skills that will elevate and accelerate your results:

START WITH QUALITY QUESTIONS – VERSUS STATEMENTS AND ANSWERS

This is key to helping your client open up, get to what really matters, and see the value you can bring them. You cannot presume to know what is most important to a client, even if you know they're about to buy servers or launch a new financial services product. That may be what they're doing, but you can be certain that is *not* the most important and valuable result to them. As it is a process or strategy, inherently they must be hoping it bridges some gap to a high-value goal or destination. Just making a purchase or making an introduction into the marketplace, in and of itself, is not a highly valuable result that produces exceptional results. You clarify their focus and enhance their perception of your value when you help them make sure their initiative succeeds in serving their highest and most important results.

Once again, it is all about finding out what is important to them. To do that, you must ask meaningful questions. We'll talk more about how to do this in the next section. For now, consider the story about winning the business of a major Fortune 500 company who was looking for training. In a 65-minute conversation, only about 15 minutes was spent describing how to achieve their high-value result and that was at the end. Most of the time was invested in asking questions to clarify, understand, reconfigure, and define the most important results they needed.

Once the high-value outcomes are clear, it is not difficult to figure out ways to achieve them. Otherwise, like the guy who spent six days trying to win their business, you are offering inadequate solutions to the wrong problems. That does not engender confidence that you are the best person to work with to achieve critically important results.

UNDERSTANDING SHORTHAND –
WHAT THEY REALLY MEAN

When somebody says, "What do you do?" they're not really asking you to describe what you do. They're using shorthand to ask you, "What do you do that has real meaning and value for me that I would really care about?"

This is why **you have to understand the real intention behind the questions someone asks you**. You have to understand their shorthand and answer what they really want to know.

Axiom #6 of The Ultimate Sales Revolution:
Make sure you understand what someone's shorthand means in order to address the real intention behind the question.

Another common shorthand is: "I'm too busy to see you." What that shorthand really means is, "I'm too busy with a whole lot of things to know whether what you're talking about has any relevance to my most important priorities, so why should I interrupt myself?"

And another, "I'm all set." That means, "I don't understand your value, your opportunity, your possibility, or the potential results that would matter to me, so I don't really see a need to add more items to my calendar."

This goes back to why it is so critical to understand the three sources of miscommunication. If you don't understand the most fundamental dynamics of human beings, then you're not going to recognize that 90 percent of the time, people are not telling you what would be most important and most valuable, and more than 99 percent of the time we really don't understand what the other person means. So when somebody says, "I'm all set," or, "I have no budget," too many people interpret that to mean, "I have no opening." In reality, **to understand what people really mean, we must facilitate clarity about what is most important to them**. That is both how we demonstrate our value to them and how we come to understand how to deliver optimal value to them.

THE SHORTHAND OF SALES

These are classic lines that every salesperson encounters and what they are shorthand for:

Shorthand: "Why should I buy from you?"

Actually Means: "Your impact, value, and results are unclear, so why should I buy from you?"

Shorthand: "I'm totally satisfied with my current vendor."

Actually Means: "I see so little differentiation between you and my current vendor, so why should I even consider changing?"

Shorthand: "I love what you have, but we don't have budget."

Actually Means: "I've allocated my budget, and either don't see your value, or it would be a hassle to change our rigid spending plan." (See how to handle this in our Troubleshooting Guide at the end of the book.)

Shorthand: "I'm not sure. Let me think about it."

Actually Means: "I hate to say no, so I'll just avoid making a decision until it doesn't matter."

Shorthand: "I need a better price."

Actually Means: "I am unclear on the value, so I need to work on the aspect I can compare – the price."

The new approach to sales in this book will have your clients saying, "Wow, these people are easy to communicate with. They actually listen – even more than they talk. They also help me get clear about what is important and do that brilliantly. I like dealing with them, trust them, and respect them. Our agendas are aligned because they're honestly trying to help me succeed, and what they're offering me is exactly what I need and not just their standard solution."

That is the only way to counter the crazy sales behavior too many salespeople exhibit and clients are repelled by. The Ultimate Sales Revolution starts with getting clients to think of you as a high-value partner, rather than all those negative words that people typically assign to sales. When clients think about you, you want them thinking about terms like *respected*, *trusted*, *open*, *communicative*, *valuable*, and *understanding* – certainly instead of *manipulation*, *coercion*, and *self-absorption*. These super-positive terms are how people refer to those who become Indispensable Partners in their success.

Becoming an Indispensable Partner requires revolution-ary, yet common-sensical, thinking and understanding. This is what clients want and welcome. This is what opens the doors to astounding success and sustainability. These are the keys to growth in your perspective, performance, and profitability. These are the shifts in thinking that cascade into massive results and rewards.

Let's look at the principles, practices, and processes needed to achieve this level of exceptional success. The next section takes you step by step through how to think and what to do to become that Indispensable Partner to your clients.

LEARNING FROM YOUR SUCCESSES AND CHALLENGES

Since you keep hearing the claim that these principles are based on fundamental, universal human dynamics, you should be able to prove them from your own experience. In fact, I guarantee that you can test and prove every one of these principles by referencing your own experience and contrasting your best and your most challenging clients. Here is what to do: Write down the names of those clients with whom you've had:

- Your best and most successful professional relationships:

    □

    □

    □

- Your most difficult and challenging professional relationships:

    □

    □

    □

As you go through the application and implementation parts of the book in the next section, test each step against these relationships. Note that each principle and practice is present with your best clients and sorely missing with your most difficult clients.

What is also noteworthy to reflect on is how you came to build the positive and successful relationships and what caused the gaps in the challenging relationships. The key leverage factors for improving every relationship are in the step-by-step process that makes up the next half of the book.

"You never change things by fighting the existing reality. To change something, build a new model that makes the existing model obsolete."

—Buckminster Fuller

PART II

SUCCESSFULLY IMPLEMENTING THE ULTIMATE SALES REVOLUTION

THE ULTIMATE SALES REVOLUTION
INDISPENSABLE PARTNER™ PROCESS

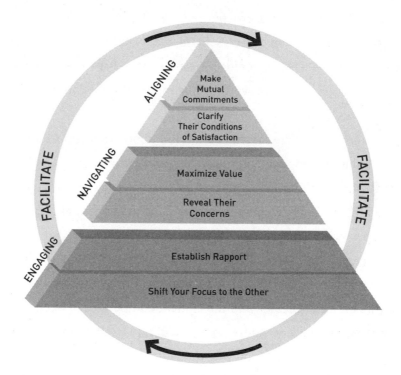

This is your map of the process for becoming an Indispensable Partner to your clients, the definitive objective of and highest accomplishment in The Ultimate Sales Revolution. It is also the highest level of professional relationship. This is the level where you massively differentiate yourself from your competition, your relationships are exceptionally rewarding, and you elevate and accelerate your success to new heights of achievement.

This section of the book gives you key principles, practices, and perspectives to achieve this highest level of professional relationship – and sales success.

The Ultimate Sales Revolution process, consisting of three stages, each with two steps, takes you, step by step, from before your first words with a prospect or client all the way to making commitments to each other about how you will work together. Each step builds on the one before it, ensuring a firm foundation for moving forward and recovering your momentum if you encounter an obstacle on the way.

Here is one important reminder about the context within which this process lives: Remember the key principle of facilitating what is most important to your clients – the critical context within which these next six steps take place – is the essential beginning of the process of creating the most outstanding communication, relationship, and results. **Remember that your role is to always facilitate clarity about what is most important as the "meta-step" in this entire process – and the critical component of each of the other six steps.** Your skillfulness and ability at effectively facilitating what is most important to your clients generates enormous leverage, impact, and conviction in you as an Indispensable Partner to them. This is the highest level of professional relationship you can achieve and the intended outcome of The Ultimate Sales Revolution process.

There are two **important perception shifts** that are critical to facilitate with your clients:

1. **Your client perceives that you understand what is most important to them**.

2. Your client perceives that you can help them take care of what is most important to them

Of course, the challenge in shift #1 is that 80 to 90 percent of the time, the clients are not even clear about what is most important to them. Remedying this lack of focus on what is most important to your clients through your facilitation gets them clear and gets you clear as well by working through the process with them.

Understanding that the first perception shift must be having your client perceive that you understand what is most important to them is different than what most salespeople do. The most common approach salespeople take is to try to get clients to understand that they can take care of the client's concerns. However, when what is most important is not yet clear, and the salesperson is focused on their offerings, it is exactly the opposite of what works best.

Building the trust, respect, communication, and relationship that characterizes the very best relationships starts with facilitating clarity about what really matters to the client. Starting here and employing the principles, practices, and skills of the Ultimate Sales Revolution will dramatically accelerate and expand your success with every client you deal with.

CHAPTER FIVE

THE STAGE OF ENGAGING

"The beginning is the most important part of the work.

—PLATO

The Principle – When you are building a high-quality relationship, you must be present and focused on your client *and* what they care about. This starts with producing a sense of connection and engagement that you must take responsibility for creating.

The Purpose – To build a quality of presence and connection with your client, which opens the door to a deeper level of communication and collaboration.

Once you recognize the essential need to become a facilitator of what is most important to your client, then the obvious next question becomes, "What do I need to do to generate that kind of engagement?"

The first stage of the journey to becoming an Indispensable Partner is Engaging. You must be able to engage with your clients and have them feel a connection to you – and it is your job to create that opening and experience. These two steps produce that outstanding level of Engaging.

STEP ONE: SHIFT YOUR FOCUS TO THE OTHER

The first thing you need to do to engage another person is to get outside your own preoccupations and off your own agenda – the "I want this to happen" kind of internal conversation. The idea is to really be present in order to: 1) listen for what is going on and 2) be able to recognize and use all the information available to you in both verbal and nonverbal ways.

Most people are so distracted much of the time that they don't really pay attention to the multiple levels of communication happening. Have you ever gone into a meeting still carrying around the last conversation you just had with your boss, your last client, or your colleague? Doing that means you're not fully present and focused on the person you're talking with. And if you're not fully present, you are not available to have full insight into what is really going on with them.

Just as importantly, when a client is talking to someone who is not fully present, what is his or her reaction? They're going to think, "This guy's here for his own interests. He's listening to himself talk. He doesn't have a clue about what I'm doing or why. Why should I care about him?" If you're not fully present, the client is not going to welcome you as a partner in their success. Furthermore, you are likely being perceived with the negative associations people already have with sales and salespeople.

Most everyone understands the value of being present. Given everything that goes on in people's lives today – the length of their to-do lists and the constant bombardment of information that we all experience – being present can be one of those things that's easier said than done.

To understand what I mean and to be more aware of potential distractions, do this simple exercise. Take 60 seconds and write down everything you need to deal with today and during this week. Once you've done that, stop and ask yourself how distracted you are. Then imagine getting a call from your biggest potential client right now. How focused would you be on his or her most important issues – one important key to demonstrating that you could be the right person for them to be working with?

This is the point: If you can't be present for the people you're talking to, why should they care about what you're talking about? You must start here. **If you truly care about the quality of your communication and relationship, you must start with being present, with and for the other person.**

CENTERED PRESENCE EXERCISE

This exercise was taught to me by my friend and martial arts master, Stuart Heller (also known as Dr. Move). In martial arts, you always need to be centered, present, and attentive. Why? Because, otherwise, you could really get hurt. It is the same in a relationship. If you're not present, attentive, and centered, your communication suffers, and your relationship will be hurt.

Research shows that more than 70 percent of judgments about somebody are made in the first seven seconds. That makes your ability to be present immediately with a person critical to being able to deepen your communication with them. I recommend that you do this exercise before you walk into any meeting with another person to ensure you are present and focused:

1. Close your eyes. With the field of your attention, find both your feet. When you've found your feet, take a deep breath.

2. Now, with the field of your attention, find both your hands. When you've found them, take a deep breath.

3. Now, with the field of your attention, find your head. When you've found it, take another deep breath.

4. Now, with the field of your attention, find both your feet and both your hands at the same time, so that the field of your attention encompasses them simultaneously. When you've done that, take a deep breath.

5. Finally, with the field of your attention, simultaneously find both your feet, both your hands, and your head. When the field of your attention encompasses all of these, take a deep breath, exhale, and open your eyes.

How centered and able to choose the direction of your attention and focus are you now?

This is something you can do anywhere – standing, sitting at your desk, wherever you are. And the more you do it, the more you can do it with extraordinary speed and effectiveness. With practice, you can do this in a split-second when you find yourself not present or focused on the people you're with. This is a simple, fast, and highly effective way to center yourself and get present with your attention.

STEP TWO: ESTABLISH RAPPORT

Being focused and present is a great start. But that just means you're here. The next step is to really build a connection with the other person, and that connection is called *rapport*. Rapport is, by dictionary definition, a sympathetic, empathetic connection with another.

Now what does sympathetic, empathetic mean exactly? It is not an intellectual or analytical process. It doesn't happen in the conscious mind. **This connection happens viscerally, in the nervous system.**

The fastest way to build this rapport, engagement, and connection is by having something in common with the other person. Given how fast people make judgments about other people, understanding the dynamics of how communication happens is extremely valuable in building that commonality and rapport.

In 1956, a UCLA professor named Albert Mehrabian published a study about how communication happens with small groups of one to four people. He tested communication on the basis of words, body language, and tone of voice. What do you think is the impact on communication from words versus tone of voice versus body language? Fill in your percentages:

- » Words: _____
- » Tone of Voice: _____
- » Body Language: _____

When I ask this of groups, the answers for what percentage of communication is represented by words typically run from 20 to 90 percent. Mehrabian claims his research showed words represent just 7 percent of communication impact. Tone of voice? Mehrabian claimed it represents 38 percent of communication. How about body language? That is fully 55 percent.

This gives us some clues as to what we need to do to find something in common and establish rapport. When you consider that 70 percent of judgments are being made in the first seven seconds, how many words can you really say in that time? Very few, so clearly finding commonality and influencing the judgments people make relies on body language and tone of voice as the levers of early communication impact and rapport.

To prove this, when speaking to groups, I'll often say in a flat tone of voice, "I'm really happy to be here today with all of you," and then I turn my back on them. Is that good communication? Of course not. Everyone knows it immediately, and I'll ask why. After all, I used the right words. However, my body language and tone of voice did not match my words. And those aspects, as we know from Mehrabian's study, hold much more weight.

Given this, **the keys to success with rapport come down to two critical factors:**

1. **Your ability to observe another**. This requires effectiveness with the prior step – being present and focused on the other person. If you're in your own mind, plotting your own agenda, fixated on your own issues, you will not be observing the other person's body language and tone of voice accurately or enough.

2. **Flexibility in your response**. Once you are willing and able to find something in common with the other person, or to do what is called "matching and mirroring," you can build rapport rapidly.

When you develop competence in these skills, you can build commonality and connection in seconds. Let's examine the power of matching and mirroring to build rapport.

MATCHING AND MIRRORING FOR FAST RAPPORT

When any of us meets someone for the first time, one of the first things we are looking for is something in common. Often that searching starts by saying something like, "Where are you from? What do you do? What brought you here?" We ask questions like that because we're looking for that something in common. And when two people who've never met before discover that they know somebody in common, it builds connection. If they discover they're from the same town or even the same state, that enhances the connection too. These people have never met each other, but they now have something in common, which is what builds that feeling of connection and opens communication.

That can work great at a cocktail party, but for professional purposes, we need a sharper, faster, more-effective way to build rapport. People are busy, and you really want to spend the bulk of your time with your clients facilitating clarity about what is most important to them. But if you're first asking them casual or random questions to build rapport, you might have to ask five or ten questions before you ever find something in common.

However, if you **understand that communication is predomi- nately influenced by our nonverbal body language and tone of voice, you can find something in common almost instantaneously by accurately observing the other person**. Once you've shifted your attention to them, then you're prepared to employ body language and tone of voice to create that commonality we seek and need for rapport.

Do you ever remember a time when you entered a crowded room, looked around, and made a connection with somebody? Something happened where you felt a connection with somebody you didn't know and had not said a thing to. That is an example of the power of body language, the single most powerful form of communication. There is something you identify with in that person's body language, which builds this empathetic, sympa- thetic connection. That makes you feel, "Ah, I like this person – we have something in common," even though you haven't said a thing to each other yet.

Matching and mirroring is the technique you can use to build this kind of rapport with someone. To do it, you have to be flexible in how you communicate, which allows you to get outside your normal mode and motion and find something in common with another person's body language and tone of voice. Maybe you're used to talking fast, but the person you're with is a slow talker. You can adjust the speed of your speech so you're talking at the same pace. You can also match the person's posture or gestures. In fact, body language is often the easiest area to match because it is something we have the capability to observe all the time. (See the "Spotting Rapport" sidebar on the next page for 24 ways to build rapport using just body language and tone of voice.)

What happens when you can't observe body language because you're on a call with someone? After all, a lot of sales happen over the phone, especially initial contacts. I'm sure you have been on a conference call where you know somebody is checking their email or doing something else. You know this because you listen to their tone of voice, and it's disengaged. Or you are attentive enough to hear their keyboard keys.

When we remove the 55 percent of communication that is body language, which is what happens when we're talking on the phone, the other aspects of communication increase proportionally to make up 100 percent. So now our tone of voice represents about 80 percent of our communication, and the words represent about 20 percent. So now tone of voice is even more critical, and it's gauged by aspects such as speed, pitch, volume, intonation, and so on. If somebody speaks really fast, and the other person responds very slowly, they are lacking commonality – and rapport. If somebody's voice is very high-pitched and the other person speaks in a bass tone, that lacks commonality too.

It is very important to remember that when you match and mirror, you don't have to change everything about you. You just need to find something in common – even one commonality can be sufficient. If you try to match everything the other person does, that could feel like mimicking. Mimicking is not what you're looking to do, is odd behavior, and can actually make people uncomfortable.

So how many things do you need in common to begin to build a connection? When I ask this question, people typically answer between three and ten. The answer is one. **You only need one communication trait in common to start building rapport**. If you're meeting somebody for the first time and find out that person lives in the same town as you, that is something in common, sufficient for building connection and rapport. Just that one thing in common is all it takes

EXERCISE: SPOTTING RAPPORT

The next time you go to a place where there are people gathered, like a restaurant, watch how people talk to each other. You will see very clearly whether they have strong rapport or not. If they have strong rapport, there are going to be many aspects of body language matching. If they don't, people will look very different. You don't even have to hear what they're saying to gauge their quality of rapport.

Following is a list of 24 ways to establish rapport using body language and tone of voice. While you're observing people, see how many of these ways you can spot:

VOICE (THE PRIMARY MEANS TO BUILDING PHONE RAPPORT)

1. Tone
2. Tempo/Rhythm
3. Pitch
4. Inflection
5. Volume

POSTURE (POSITION OF THE BODY)

6. Head
7. Neck
8. Shoulders
9. Arms
10. Torso
11. Body balance

BODY LANGUAGE (MOVEMENT)

12. Facial expressions
13. Body movements
14. Rhythm
15. Hand movements
16. Shoulders
17. Gestures
18. Legs
19. Arms
20. Head

BREATHING

21. Depth
22. Fullness
23. Frequency
24. Loudness

WHAT HAPPENS IF YOU LOSE RAPPORT?

What can you do if you're present and ready to build rapport with someone and that person isn't? We live in a world today where people are constantly multitasking and quite distracted. You may walk into a meeting with someone and they have their cellphone out. Or maybe, instead of looking at you, they're distracted by what is on their computer screen. Is there something you can do to help that person focus on what is most important to them?

Of course there is. You can match and mirror them, creating something in common with body language and/or tone of voice. That doesn't mean that if the person is on their cellphone that you get out yours and do the same. Remember, you have to be present, observe them, and match one or two aspects of body language to build rapport. It can be something as simple as matching the tilt of their head, the position of their shoulders, or the movement of their hands.

Test this using your own common sense and experience. Suppose you're in client services at a hotel, and a guest comes to the desk irate because there was no hot water in the shower. He is intense and ranting, "Do you know how much I paid for this room and there is no hot water?" If you soothingly say to him, "Please calm down, sir. I'd be happy to help you with that," what is the message being communicated with your tone of voice? You don't get it!

You've said the right words, but to the guest, you don't appear to understand how significant this is to him. Your tone of voice, body language, and way of speaking doesn't reflect an understanding of the magnitude of this issue to him. There is a complete mismatch between you and the guest. So what happens as a result? The guest amps up his intensity even further, because to him you just don't understand how important this is.

What do people typically do when they are not being understood? Whether it's a seemingly uncaring hotel clerk or someone in a foreign country who doesn't speak your language, the response is typically the same; the misunderstood person increases the intensity of their body language and the volume of their speech – even though they were not understood the first time.

Imagine instead that you match that guest's intensity but without matching his emotionality and anger. Instead of saying, "Please calm down," you can say, with some intensity, "That's absolutely terrible. It is unacceptable, and I apologize. Let me take care of this for you right away!" Now your body language, tone of voice, *and* your words communicate that you get it. You have successfully matched and mirrored him, the communication was successful, and now the guest can cool down a bit.

What we're talking about here is not matching bad energy, emotion, or action; it is about finding something in common. You don't have to be angry or upset to amp up your language and body language and communicate that you understand that what is important to that person is important to you too.

IT JUST TAKES ONE

When leading seminars on this subject, I have used a dramatic exercise to drive home the power of matching and mirroring. The group is split in half, and one group goes into the hall, while the other stays in the room. The members of the hall group are asked to come up with something they're passionate about that they can discuss for two minutes. I then tell the members of the group in the room, "When the first group comes in and starts talking, for the first minute, mismatch them. If they're leaning forward, you lean back. If they're speaking quickly, you speak slowly. If they're using their hands, you keep your hands down." I tell them not to be aggressive, just different. Then, after the first minute, I tell this group to switch gears and start matching and mirroring the other person.

The results are remarkable to watch. The level of disconnection in the first minute is immense. After that first minute, the volume and energy more than doubles when everybody starts matching, mirroring, and building rapport. After two minutes are up, I ask the people who were talking – who had no idea what instructions the other group had been given – what their experience was like. All around the world, people respond with the same comments, "I didn't even want to talk to him at first. I was really insulted. She didn't care. She wasn't even listening. He was totally disinterested."

When asked, "Was it like that for the whole time?" they always say, "No, it changed about halfway through." When asked, "What did you do to create that change?" people respond with things like, "Well, I just kept trying, or asked questions, or tried to make her laugh, and finally, after about a minute, she came around."

I also ask the other group what it felt like to mismatch someone for just one minute. People always say, "That was really hard. I felt terrible and uncomfortable, like I was hurting them or I was ignoring them, and I could see they were upset. I didn't like it at all." What happened when they started matching and mirroring? "It was great. Everything took off from there, we got reconnected, had an excellent conversation from that point, and everything felt good."

The lessons of this exercise are critically important**. If you don't have rapport, people are disconnected, unhappy, and can feel insulted**. They experience that you're not listening, you don't care, they don't matter, nothing that they're saying is important, and you're not the kind of person that they want to be with.

Also critically important to understand is that **you can change that instantaneously by using all these aspects of communication**

to build a strong rapport. As important, you can do that all on your own. **Just one person's intention made the difference between having a terrible connection and a good one**.

Axiom #7 of The Ultimate Sales Revolution:
It only takes one skilled and committed person to build rapport.

ENGAGING WITH CONTEXT SETTING

Another important aspect of building a strong engagement is context setting, which is analogous to choosing a frame for a picture. Imagine you've got different pictures or paintings on the walls in your house. If you frame them differently, they'll look and feel very different. An ornate gold frame has a different impact than a plain wooden one or an elegant silver one. The frame itself changes how the picture looks.

By the same token, the context in which you start a conversation affects how that conversation looks and feels to the other person. Think back to the story I told in Chapter 2 about the difference seven minutes can make. After that buyer said she did not want to see me, she opened up when she heard, "Would you be willing to invest seven minutes to examine how this could help your program be even better and more successful?" I didn't say, "Can I have seven minutes of your time?"

There is a big difference between those two conversation starters. The context of the first one is that she could be even more successful. The context of the second is that I want to take her time. Which is more appealing – and compelling – to the other person?

That kind of opening really engages the listener, setting the tone or context for the entire conversation. Suppose you're meeting with a CFO who says, "I want the lowest price." You might respond with: "How open are you to considering the implications on your revenue, profitability, and success of other aspects, including reliability, on-time delivery, and quality, in addition to getting a highly competitive price?" By responding like that, you change the context. By framing the conversation differently, you're shifting their focus to all the aspects of success, not just price. Consider how that positions you as a very valuable partner in helping them achieve the highest levels of success.

Setting context is another way to build connection and engagement with someone. You're showing them that you're focused on them and what is really important to them. That makes the other person think, "Wow, this is the kind of person I like to deal with – someone who has my best interests at heart and expands my thinking and capability for success."

An important note about setting context is that the more you know about the other person and what is important to them, the more you can frame the conversation in ways that connect with what really matters to them. With new clients, that takes some research and preparation. There is a lot of information about people available today with LinkedIn, Facebook, informational databases, and the like. It behooves us all to find out as much as we can before meeting someone so we can find those points of connection to what is really important to them.

THE POWER OF RAPPORT

The power of rapport is profound. It is one of the most underrated and most critically important points of leverage for building an Indispensable Partner relationship. **Great rapport and engagement opens the door to deeper communication**. Imagine that strong rapport is like opening the garage door to the house where their deeper concerns and objectives can be found. It's that much of an opening.

To open that door, it is important to make sure that the person feels connected to you. Without strong rapport and connection, they won't share what really matters to them. They must get that you're there for their best interests and feel a level of connection, or the door to their real concerns remains closed.

Think about going to a doctor, lawyer, or financial planner who comes across as arrogant and treats you like they're so expert you should just let them do what they want and not worry about it. That's not the person you want to work with, even when your health, legal, or financial well-being is at risk. When clients are talking to somebody selling services, it's the same thing. The first order of business becomes, do I trust this person? Do I believe that he or she really is the kind of person who will understand me and take care of my best interests? If the answer is not a resounding yes, then you have a nearly insurmountable wall to get over.

Once you have engaged them with rapport, you'll see how much information and insight the other person will offer up. You'll find an extraordinary level of attunement when you're observant of their body language, listening to their tone of voice, and attentive to their words. You'll also be able to gauge the person's level of commitment by their tone of voice and their body language when they answer your questions.

So often we take words at face value, but they are the easiest things to manipulate. It is much harder for people to disguise their real feelings expressed through their body language and tone of voice. Those are far better barometers of whether someone is committed to their answers or just telling us what they think we want to hear to get us to move on.

You can start to see why this stage of engaging is so critical to becoming an Indispensable Partner. When someone is talking about what really matters to them, too many salespeople miss it because they're thinking their own thoughts, they're interpreting what they hear, and they're not present and paying attention to the client's tone of voice and body language.

For example, when somebody tells you four things that matter to them, common sense tells us that those four things are not of equal importance. Generally, among the four, one is going to be most important, another is second most important, and so on. If you watch the person's body language and listen to their tone of voice – the energetic impact and emphasis as someone talks – you can understand a tremendous amount. You can often identify which of those four matters most by the way they talk about them.

That is the power of rapport. It gives you massive connection to another person so that they feel connected and want to communicate with you. **Rapport opens the door to deeper communication and relationship and gives you tremendous insight and nuanced understanding about what somebody cares about.** This happens only if you're really present with them, observing them, and listening to them, and if you avoid getting caught up in your own preoccupations and interpretations about what they are saying.

If you look back at the Indispensable Partner pyramid, this is your base camp. This stage is the foundation you need to build to accomplish everything else. Now, a lot of people are pretty good at engaging. It is a basic human characteristic to want to be connected to other people, and, typically, successful salespeople have a pretty good capacity to connect. However, if you're committed to being the best and most successful, then pretty good is insufficient. What you are learning here are the keys to the *most outstanding* quality of connection and engagement with your clients. And that starts with:

1. Being present with people and focused on them.

2. Making sure that people really feel a visceral, sympathetic, empathetic connection with you.

Someone who does these well is trusted by the client far more than a person who just says the right things. High-quality engagement is too rare today. You will note that it is almost completely missing with your most challenging clients.

Building outstanding engagement is the essential opening to far deeper and more-powerful communication and relationship. Done well, this already starts to set you apart from most of your competition.

TURNING PRINCIPLES INTO PRACTICE

SKILL BUILDING: HANDLING TOUGH
BUSINESS SITUATIONS

List one of the most challenging situations that you are currently dealing with or have encountered. Consider how you might handle it differently using the principles, skills, and techniques learned so far.

Briefly describe the current or past situation you have chosen to focus on.

What makes, or made, this situation difficult or challenging?

What could you do to approach it differently, or what could you have done differently?

What principles and skills would you or could you employ?

CHAPTER SIX

THE STAGE OF NAVIGATING

"If you don't know where you are going, you'll end up someplace else."

—YOGI BERRA

The Principle – Just like if you were on a journey, to reach your destination of building a high-value relationship with a client, you must keep two things clear:

1. Where the client is at the moment.

2. Their destination or desired outcome.

Only then can you make the choices necessary to chart the path from where they are to their destination. These two points must always be clear to you, as obstructions and modifications are often going to force changes in your path.

The Purpose – Knowing your client's high-value outcomes is key to ultimate success. Knowing where the client "is" and what they're focused on at any moment is also critical. Ensuring there is agreement with your client on both these points is the starting point for effectively navigating toward and attaining that desired destination.

The second stage of being an Indispensable Partner is navigating. To understand this, consider a story about working with the FAA. As senior executives were escorting me around their DC headquarters, they told me, "When you fly, you're off course 98 percent of the time." That might be a scary thought, except if you really understand how navigation works. After all, flying with the top 39 airlines in the world, your chances of being in a fatal accident over the last 20 years is 1 in 10 million. Navigation is a critical skill for pilots – and anyone who needs to influence another person.

The three things pilots need to keep in mind to navigate successfully are:

1. They need to always know where they are.

2. They need to always know where their destination is.

3. They always need to be finding the best path to navigate between these two points.

Whether you're a pilot, a sailor, or you're climbing a mountain, if you don't know where you are, then it is impossible to figure out how to get to your destination. By the same token, if you don't know what the destination is, as the Mad Hatter says in *Alice in Wonderland*, "Then any path will do." But any path won't do for us, because we're committed to the path of being an Indispensable Partner in our client's success.

What that means is we need to understand where the client is and where they really need to be going. Remember that most of the time where they think they're going is not where it would be most valuable for them to end up.

In aviation, you might run into storms, winds, equipment issues, passenger issues, or any number of unforeseeable situations. By always knowing where you are and your destination, you can figure out how to navigate around whatever comes up and get where you really wanted to go. If you're flying from New York to San Francisco, it is not going to be a straight line. You're going to make adjustments along the way depending on what comes up. It is the same with relationships and delivering meaningful results to clients.

We need to be able to navigate with clients by knowing where they are and by knowing their most important destination. If we don't understand what the most important destination is, then any path will do – and we could end up hundreds of miles, or hundreds of thousands of dollars, off course. If we facilitate clarity about what really matters to clients, it is not that difficult to continually build and navigate the most efficient path to get there.

There are two more factors to navigation. One is that it is important to monitor the quality of your progress toward your high-value destination. This is not about monitoring the specifications – a critical distinction. I'm talking about monitoring progress toward the destination, which is what matters most. Too many people get diverted into managing specifications and activities. Delivering high-impact and valuable results requires keeping the most important outcomes in your sights and tracking your progress, especially because often factors and situations change.

The other important factor is to make modifications to get to your destination as they become necessary. For example, historically, a majority of IT projects come in late. What typically ends up happening is the provider of a multimillion-dollar IT project that is going to come in late feels like a failure, and the client is not happy because they don't have 20 percent of the specifications that were agreed to at the outset. When working with a major corporation on their IT projects, here is what we would do instead: We made sure we understood the client's most important results. Then we prioritized our activities to deliver those highest-priority results first. So while we may have only delivered 80 percent of the specifications by a certain date, we were delivering 97 or 98 percent of the high-value results that the clients needed. This delivered virtually everything the client really needed and took the pressure off the IT group. The client was thrilled to get the high-value results, and the IT team could then finish up the other 20 percent of specifications that delivered only 2 or 3 percent of the value with a strong sense of satisfaction and accomplishment.

Delivering 97 percent of the desired functionality and results to your client is totally different than saying you failed to deliver 20 percent of the specifications. But, in order to do that, **the focus for your client and you must be on the important results**. This also demonstrates that you have been smart and attentive enough with your clients to deliver 97 percent of the value the client needed on time. Which do you think a client would be happier about – meeting the specifications or achieving the functionality and results? It's the latter, of course, and this shows why we must start with clarity right in the beginning.

This comes back to the story in Chapter 1 about the $8 million disaster, where three years of work got thrown away. That project was being driven by a 100-plus page book of specifications, which no one on the project looked up from long enough to ask the really important questions: "Is our destination valuable, high impact, and still meaningful?" and, "Are we getting there in the best and most appropriate ways, especially given everything going on in the business and in new technology development?"

Navigating to a high-value destination should be a continuous process, but it wasn't for that company. The agenda they set in the beginning was focused more on process than results, and then they buried their heads in the process. If they had been monitoring their high-value results and the changes in the market and technology all along, they would have realized that there were dramatic changes going on all around them, which altered the high-value destination. They needed to continuously make the necessary adjustments so that when the project was finished, the results and the technology delivered what the client needed most.

It was a very costly lesson to learn – the importance of focusing on the most valuable and important impact, value, and results that the client really needed, as well as what was going on around them in the market that could affect those critical results. Success starts with the very first conversation and clarification about what the critical results need to be. It must continue all the way to the delivery of the prioritized outcomes that give the client the impact, value, and results they really need.

STEP THREE: REVEAL THE CLIENT'S CONCERNS

Once you have a strong engagement, the next step is to facilitate clarity about the concerns of your client. This is a natural progression in human relationships – once you have a connection or engagement with someone, you want to know more about them and their "concerns." In this context concerns mean what has their attention – which could be thoughts, feelings, or ideas – and is driving their decision-making.

It is through these concerns that you can help them discern and focus on what the most important and valuable results could be. Of course you want to ensure that you are navigating toward high-impact results and not just details or specifications. Results are the "coin of the realm" as an Indispensable Partner in your clients' success. **Helping them get clear in this way involves taking what they are focused on and elevating toward valuable, high-impact results.**

We already know that people tend to *not* focus on, make the best decisions about, nor articulate well what is really most important as much as 90 percent of the time. Even if they are giving you clear and compelling outcomes, you need to test that these are the most valuable outcomes worth focusing on. That is how we become facilitators of what is most important to them, by really helping them have clarity about and focus on that.

To do this, we must understand how people think, evaluate, and make their decisions. By understanding and being proficient with facilitating how humans function at their best, your capacity for effectiveness and being your client's Indispensable Partner increases dramatically.

Human beings think, decide, evaluate, and make their decisions based on what I call their concerns. Someone's concerns could encompass their biggest problems, their biggest challenges, their biggest opportunities, their biggest hopes, their biggest fears, their biggest desires, what their boss told them they wanted, what their organization claims really matters, and so forth. All of these are concerns or what has their attention.

The concerns that have someone's attention could be positive or negative. They could be self-generated or externally generated. Either way, they grab their attention and influence their focus. By the way, they may have nothing to do with what is really most important or essential to their success.

Suppose you're a financial advisor, and after reviewing someone's portfolio you say, "Those are not the best investments for you. Let me work up the best approach to get you the results you really want." How would that person respond?

The prospect might agree, even though they're not sure why they need to change their portfolio, because as the expert, you didn't explain it well. Then, at the end of the year, they find they're no better off than where they were in the first place. Given the presumptuousness, lack of clarity, and failure to deliver meaningful results, they wouldn't work with you again.

Here is the Indispensable Partner approach: you walk in and start by asking the prospective client some context-setting and clarifying questions. "What are the most important results you desire? What are your biggest challenges and greatest opportunities? What would you value most in this process?" After you have facilitated that discussion, they would come to a better understanding of their priority outcomes. That's a superior way to build the relationship and get to what is most important.

Once their concerns and most important results are clear to them, then they are ready for this discussion: "Are you certain that you are pursuing the best approach to get your results? How open are you to an alternative that would be more aligned with your concerns, expectations, as well as your desired results?"

Your greatest impact comes when you facilitate and help clients see the possibilities and results from working with you – in addition to building the trust, respect, and open communication essential for the best relationship. **The difference between facilitating someone to understand for himself or herself what is most important and telling them what you want them to know has magnitudes – not percentages – more impact.**

Axiom #8 of The Ultimate Sales Revolution:
It is worth more than ten times as much to facilitate your client seeing, understanding, and saying what is most important and valuable, as for you to tell them what it is (even if you are right).

GETTING TO WHAT REALLY MATTERS
– AND PROVING YOUR VALUE

One of the fundamentals taught in old-school sales training is fact finding. Salespeople are told to get all the facts, like the client's budget, timeframe, company statistics, or other factual information. The facts are generally available to anyone who will ask the questions, "What is your budget?" or, "What is your deadline?"

In practicing sales as an Indispensable Partner, what you need to learn how to do is use your client's opinions. The reason is that **a person's opinions are their representations of how they think, evaluate, and make their decisions**. **These are the access points for revealing what is most important to them.**

For example, what happens if I ask three different people, "How are things going today?" I'm going to get three different answers, likely with words and certainly with tone of voice and body language: "It's great," "It's okay," and "It's fine." These answers or opinions they're giving describing their day are their representations of how they're evaluating and thinking about the day.

If I asked three leaders, "What are the most important results in your organization," and one said, "increased sales," another said, "increased profits," and the third said, "increased client retention," am I learning about the most important results in the business, or am I learning about how these people think about and evaluate their business? It's the latter, of course. When somebody gives an opinion, we're seeing their representation of how they think about, evaluate, and make their decisions about particular issues or topics.

What is powerful to understand is that at the deepest levels of a person's thinking, evaluating, and decision making, there is enormous consistency. They may not be conscious about these deeper drivers, but an opinion they give you is going to be based on these.

This is a fundamental, critically important aspect of human dynamics. By facilitating and helping a client understand their fundamental thinking, evaluation, and decision-making process, you can help your client gain greater clarity and focus on their most important concerns and outcomes.

To influence you in the deepest and most profoundly powerful way, do we just accept what you say – which we know 90 percent of the time is not connected to what is most important? The best option is to ensure that the thinking, evaluation, and decision making is coherently aligned with and connected to what is most important. That is also a dramatic demonstration of the value that someone will get working with a person who is so dedicated to and so effective at getting to what is most important and valuable.

Essentially, **you help them define the high value outcome as well as the gap between where they are and where they really want and need to be. This creates that critical perception shift where they know you know what is most important to them – because you elegantly helped them get there!**

The key understanding in helping them get crystal clear is knowing that **facilitating with their opinions is magnitudes more powerful than collecting their facts.**

◊ Axiom #9 of The Ultimate Sales Revolution:
The greatest cause of miscommunication is not knowing the difference between facts and opinions.

What is the real difference between facts and opinions, and why does it really matter? A fact is something that can be validated as right or wrong, correct or not. An opinion is a personal expression reflecting someone's thinking, evaluations, and beliefs.

If you listen to our political discourse today, people often frame their opinions as if they're facts. You might hear someone say: "The President is a [blank]." Fill in the blank however you want, but almost all the time it is an opinion.

"Babe Ruth is the best who ever played baseball." Fact or opinion?

Opinion.

"The Yankees are the best team to ever play." They've won 27 World Series Championships – a fact – but being the best is just pure opinion.

If we hear someone give an opinion like this, do we learn something about the subject they are talking about, or do we learn more about the person expressing the opinion?

"This is an outstanding program producing spectacular results" has to be an opinion, since there is no objective definition of an outstanding program or of spectacular results.

When we hear opinions, it is an outstanding gateway to learning about the person speaking. Using these powerful insights well is critically important if you are committed to becoming an Indispensable Partner.

Many people haven't stopped to understand the profound difference between a client's facts and opinions. When you're talking with a client, what you really want to understand – and help them see – is their best thinking, evaluating, and decision making.

When you can influence that process, you'll have massively more leverage and impact than you would by just trying to manipulate your offering to fit what they say they want. Getting a person to share their opinions is how you access their thinking, evaluation, and decision-making processes. It builds trust, openness, and access to what really matters. It also allows you to ensure that what they're asking for is consistent with and will deliver what is most important, valuable, and meaningful to them. That further cements their trust in and respect for the value you are delivering already.

USING OPINIONS – AND THE VOLCANO MODEL

To help you appreciate the differential in the power of opinions versus the underlying and far

FACTS VS. OPINIONS

FACTS

- Can always be tested for veracity.
- Imply a commitment to provide proof that the claim is true, if requested.
- Are based on universally accepted standards, authorities, or judgments.

OPINIONS

- Do not describe anything factually.
- Are based upon personal interpretation.
- Are useful for revealing the evaluation standards of the person issuing the opinion.
- Can help to reveal someone's concerns through further questioning.
- Are often confused with facts because they are delivered with an emphatic tone of voice and body language.

more powerful basis for those opinions, consider the metaphor of an erupting volcano.

When a volcano erupts, it always starts by spewing steam, gas, and dust. Now, that really looks significant, right? However, what it really tells us is that there is something far more important and powerful going on inside. It is easy to get caught up in the intensity of the steam, dust, and gas. However, those elements are quickly rendered insignificant when the volcano erupts, spewing lava.

In the context of communication, opinions are like the steam and dust coming out of a volcano. They sound pretty significant, especially when they're intense and strong. However, what they really tell us is that there is something far more significant going on inside of that person, at the source of those opinions.

Understanding the human dynamics in this situation, you know real value will come, for you and for them, far faster when you can connect them to the basis of their opinions. That is their thinking, evaluating, and decision-making foundations, which are far sounder sources of meaningful decisions than their opinions ever could be.

OPINIONS AS REPRESENTATIONAL SYSTEMS

Let's look more deeply at how opinions operate as a representational system for a person's thinking and decision-making structure. **Every opinion somebody gives you, especially a strong opinion, is a representation of his or her deepest thinking, evaluation, and decision-making process and structure.**

However, that opinion can still be disconnected from or misaligned with their most important and high-impact results. People often request something because they're frustrated, harried, their boss demanded it, or they're under pressure. Therefore, they're not thinking deeply or specifically about what is most important. Instead, they're thinking, "How the heck do I get this off my to-do list?"

Your job is to facilitate clarity about what their opinion really means and represents, all the way down to what is most important. Look at the opinions being expressed as if they are attached via a rope to the deepest and most valuable criteria someone would really want to base their decision on. You want to find where that rope connects to the most fundamental, most important criteria for their thinking, evaluation, and decision making.

Once you understand the significance and potential value of someone's opinion, using a well-structured questioning strategy is like having the keys to a vault filled with gold.

This questioning strategy, naturally, is built on an understanding of human dynamics. We know that when someone offers an opinion, it is probably not really what is ultimately most important. Suppose a client says to you, "We need a new strategic plan." You could say, "We're the best strategic planning people around. Let us come in, and we'll develop your strategic plan," and then you do that, leaving them with a brilliant strategic plan. The chances are very strong that six months later, you would go back and discover that their people are confused, and their strategy is stalled. This happens too often in business.

Here is the way to respond to a client asking for a new strategic plan: "Let's assume you had the best possible strategic plan, and it was working brilliantly. What critical results would you be able to achieve?" Is the key issue the plan, or is it the important results? You know the answer.

You frame the question essentially the same way every time. A client says, "I need leadership development." You ask: "What are the most important results you're working to achieve with your leadership development?"

"I need a new IT system." Really? Because no one really needs a new IT system. What they need are the decision-making capabilities from better information generated faster or presented in ways that allow them to make critical decisions. So you ask: "What are the most important results you're trying to achieve with your IT system?"

You get the picture. **Whenever the client gives you an opinion about what they think they need, you have a massive opening to facilitate a deeper level of insight, awareness, and importance that comes from using an opinion well.**

Your job is to use their opinions to help them go deeper and clarify what's really most important, valuable, and meaningful. If you were to give the client the IT system they asked for, you're likely going to fail to deliver maximum value, for one simple yet profound reason: **no process or action is ever going to be as valuable as the results that it can generate**. In this more-successful world of sales, focus on what is most valuable, meaningful, and significant to your client and their company – critically important   results.

Axiom #10 of The Ultimate Sales Revolution:
Results are ALWAYS far more valuable than the processes that generate them.

4-STEP QUESTIONING STRATEGY FOR REVEALING CONCERNS

(Note: X = Opinion; A, B, C = Values)

1: Get an opinion from the other person – ideally a strong opinion.

What This Brings Forth: This opens the door to their decision-making process – the stronger the opinion, the easier it is to access a deeper level.

Questions to Use:

- What do you think about 'X'?
- What do you like most about 'X'?
- What do you like least about 'X'?

2: Find out what the opinion represents to them – then do it again and do it again until you get to a deep level of what is really important to them.

What This Brings Forth: Understanding of the deeper decision-making and evaluation criteria by which their decisions are made.

Questions to Use:

- What do you mean it is 'X'?
- What about 'X' did you like?
- What would 'X' give you?
- What is most important to you about 'X'?

3: Understand their hierarchy – or priority order – of concerns and values.

What This Brings Forth: Showing their hierarchy of decision-making helps get them connected in a conscious way to their own most important criteria.

Questions to Use:

- Would you say A is more important than B? (if no – ask if B is more important than A).

- While it seems A, B and C are important to you – which would you say are most important in making this decision?

4: Make sure they are viscerally as well as intellectually in touch with and associated with what is most important to them.

What This Brings Forth: It helps them make their decisions congruently with their hierarchy of values, involving them viscerally and intellectually.

Questions to Use:

- If we delivered A, B, and C – how satisfied would you be?

- What must happen for you to be confident that you have A, B, and C?

STEP FOUR: MAXIMIZING VALUE

Now that you understand how to get to what is really important, your next job is to look at how you get the client to the level of their deepest thinking or "e-value-ation."

Note that the word "value" is at the core of *evaluation*. A value is what is most important to experience or feel – the states of being that people most want. Gaining clarity about what is most important and valued provides the strongest focus and raises the level of dialogue to a much higher level. It is also crucial to establish multiple ways that you can deliver on what your clients want most, prior to acting on them. This is about really helping people make the best decisions to serve their highest and best capabilities, impact, value, and results.

Getting to a client's values is extraordinarily useful and powerful for the following reasons:

☐ Values determine a person's focus.

☐ Depending on what people are focused on, they could end up engaging around actions (rules) or what is most important (values).

☐ The best decisions are based on what is most important to someone – what they value.

☐ Poor decisions, or decisions that do not serve people well, are nearly always the result of not taking into consideration what is most important and valuable.

MEANS VALUES VERSUS ENDS VALUES

There is a critical differentiation to be made between means and ends values. To understand the difference, start by examining the answer to a question, "Would you like to make more money?" When I ask this of a group, everybody raises their hand. Then when asked, "Would you like to double your income?" Everybody enthusiastically says, "Yes. Of course."

Then I continue, "If you want to make more money, there is a job available where you can do this. It's an important job, and it pays twice as much as you're making now, but you have to understand what you're getting into. You've got to commit to this job for at least two years, and you need to know – it's incredibly boring. You'll be doing the exact same thing for eight to ten hours a day, every day, but it's an important job that you'll be well compensated for. Do you still want it?"

When put that way to the groups I work with, every single person declines. These are typically high-performing professionals who value challenge, growth, excitement, and learning. These are the ends values that successful people want in their lives.

More money is important too, but most people aren't willing to sacrifice the experiences they want and value most just to make more money.

The key understanding from this is that money is a thing. Status is a thing. Family is a thing. We tend to get very attached to things like these, but these things are actually just a means to an end.

Take, for example, family. Just about everyone holds family to be important. When working with groups, I'll often ask four volunteers to write down what is most important to them about family. The structure of that question is very important: "What is most important to you about [blank]." You can fill in the blank with whatever thing you're interested in – family, job, money, the project you are currently working on. Whatever it is, the structure of the question is designed to get you value-oriented answers.

Here is what might surprise you: I've never had four people give the exact same answers to the question, "What is most important to you about family?" The kinds of answers that people come up with are values like security, support, love, compassion, caring, connection, contribution, engagement, delight, meaning, and fun. Family means a set of ends values that are specific to each person.

After getting the answers, I'll ask the volunteers, "Which do you really want most? The love, caring, and support that you said were most important to you about family? Or this thing you call family? You can either have that thing you call family or those feelings you associate with family, but you can't have both. Which do you choose?"

All of a sudden, the answer changes. People begin to realize that what they really want is the love, caring, and support that they associate with family, not this thing called family. Family, then, is a means to an end. And the end – the love, caring, and support – is what is really most important to people.

Most people don't recognize the difference between means and ends values. Here is why the distinction matters so much. Suppose you're talking to a client, and they say that family is most important to them. Well then, you have no way of giving them what they want. However, if you understand that what they really value about family are the feelings of caring and support that they associate with it, then you have an opportunity to provide those even more important ends-value experiences. You are not their family, but you can provide caring and support. Now you've gone from not being able to give the client what they want to being able to deliver something even more important than that thing they initially said they cared most about.

Let's take another example that's more common in the world of sales – money. Like family, money is a thing, so the question becomes, what is most important to you about money? Typical answers are ends values such as freedom, security, adventure, excitement, respect, and recognition. Different people will have different answers that show what ends-values money is a means to for them.

After explaining this, a client jumped up one time, recognizing how he lost one of his best people over the ends- versus means-values confusion. His top associate demanded more money, saying, "If you don't give me more money, I'm leaving." So he arranged, in very tight financial times, a $25,000 raise. It wasn't easy, but he did it. And that person still left three weeks later. That was a clear demonstration that it wasn't about the money.

Money was just the means to something even more important that this employee wasn't getting. Even with this substantial $25,000 raise – clearly a means value – he left. What was lacking was an understanding of what was really important to that associate. Without that knowledge, it would be nearly impossible to satisfy him – even though money is what he claimed he needed to stay. Once again, what was asked for was not what was most important, and it did not produce a satisfying outcome for anyone.

That's why it is critical to know the difference between means values and ends values.

Had this manager understood what his employee was really asking for when he said he wanted more money, he might have been able to be more effective. Maybe the employee was really looking for more recognition and respect. The boss could have provided that, and, if understood as the real desired outcome, would actually have been easier to provide – and more effective – than the $25,000 raise.

That's another critical point to recognize here. **There is a massive difference between the effort you have to make with means values and the impact you can have with ends values**. To become part of your family, for example, isn't really possible. Plus, it wouldn't really give you what is most important to you. To give you more money may be extremely high effort but not necessarily high value, as it was in this particular case where the employee ended up leaving anyway. However, when I understand that the ends values you really care about is not money but recognition and respect, and not family but caring and support, multiple ways to deliver that to you can be arranged more easily. I can massively increase the value and impact and dramatically decrease the effort it takes.

This is the power of differentiating between means and ends values. The actions or things that means values demand can require massive effort and difficulty with low value and impact. But by delivering the ends values someone really seeks, you can provide massive value and impact with less effort and difficulty. **Getting to a client's ends values allows you to more easily deliver what matters most. It also produces a dramatic reinforcement of how good and valuable you can be for your client or employees because of your ability to get to what really matters, while avoiding being derailed with low value requests.**

VALUE-BASED QUESTION: WHAT IS MOST IMPORTANT TO YOU ABOUT...?

NINJA COMMUNICATION SKILLS

Looking back at the questioning strategy in the last section, remember that what we're doing is leveraging opinions to get to what is really most valuable and important. When somebody says, "I need it faster, and I need it cheaper," that's an opinion. There is no fact there. You can get to the real ends value behind that opinion by asking the value-based question: "What is most important to you about (in this case) having it faster and cheaper?"

When asking a question like that, you need to be engaged, present, focused on the client, and have excellent rapport in order to get the quality of answer that elevates the conversation (all the steps we have covered to this point). If the client recognizes that you're there for their best interests and working to help them get clear and focused on what would have the greatest impact, value, and results, you'll get the best, honest, and thoughtful answers that will drive the most immense impact and value.

Think about the difference between that kind of values-based question and asking an old-fashioned, open-ended question like, "Tell me more about what you need." Which better demonstrates you are there for them? Which is going to get you to the most valuable, highest impact, most important result faster?

As you're having this kind of communication with the client, there are ways you can keep them focused on what is most important. Let's call these ninja communication skills. First, you can help them open up their thinking and get outside the usual biggest obstacle, which is not knowing how to accomplish something they want to do. If someone says, "I need it cheaper than before," **help them go beyond that obstacle by imagining the problem has already been resolved.** Ask: "Imagine you've already got it as cheap as you wanted – what would that give you?" This moves the focus of the conversation from a means value and helps you get to a high-value end result. You want this dialogue to be all about what is most important about that action or thing they want.

The second ninja communication skill is to **use superlatives to help people quickly and effectively distill their thinking.** You don't have to collect 100 answers from someone. What you really want are the highest-priority, most important results they really value. For example, instead of asking, "What do you like about your current vendor?" which could result in a whole laundry list of answers, ask, "What do you like *most* about your current vendor?"

There really is a different feeling in those two questions, and the latter is going to lead to a simpler, clearer, yet higher-value answer. By using superlatives, you give people a process where they can quickly and more effectively distill their best thinking.

THE VALUE OF VALUES

These are simply ways to get clients to express opinions, because you know that those opinions are connected to what is really important. **When you help your clients get to what is most important, you're going to have much more clarity about what is really worth doing together. This is also the best way to build trust, respect, and great communication, as well as demonstrate the value they get with you – *before* you've even talked about your**

products or services. This is critical because it powerfully differ-entiates you from your competition, who tends to talk about what they have and do.

As a salesperson, you must immediately and clearly demonstrate your value and instill confidence that you can deliver what is most important. Otherwise, how do they know how valuable you can be?

One of the questions every salesperson should think about is, "When do you determine your price?" Price should be based on your value. But you are going to negotiate your price before you've ever delivered anything. How do your clients assess your value before they've actually seen you do what you do? Before you have delivered any of your products or services?

Your demonstration, from the very first conversation, that you can get a client clear, focused, and committed to what is most important, valuable, and of highest impact to them is your ultimate value demonstration. It builds everything that you need for an outstanding relationship and satisfies the first law of being a facilitator: They must perceive that you know what is most important to them. **Facilitating them to clarity about what is most important is the ultimate validation that you know what matters and you are going to be effective in delivering it. Already you've established a massive value proposition. That's how you maximize your value and differentiate yourself from your competition.**

PUTTING IDEAS INTO PRACTICE

TEST YOURSELF: COMPARING YOUR BEST AND MOST CHALLENGING RELATIONSHIPS

QUESTIONS:

1. Considering your most successful relationship(s):

   a. How well do you know what is most important to them?

   b. What is it?

   c. When you are discussing how you are going to fulfill what is most important with them, what is the ratio of discussing results/outcomes with them versus discussing specification and actions?

2. Consider your most difficult and challenging relationship(s):

   a. How well do you know what is most important to them?

   b. What is it?

   c. What must you do to increase the discussion and focus on results and outcomes with them versus discussing specification and actions?

3. What makes your best relationship work so well?

4. What makes your challenging relationship so difficult?

5. What is your most important learning from this exercise?

CHAPTER SEVEN

THE STAGE OF ALIGNING

"If I had an hour to save the world, I would spend 59 minutes defining the problem and one minute finding solutions."

—ALBERT EINSTEIN

The Principle – The Stage of Aligning is about making sure that your actions clearly deliver what is most important to the client. Therefore, before you take any action, you must understand what is most important to the client (accomplished in the Stage of Navigation). This is the only way to ensure that your actions will have impact and value. If you are not clear about what is most important, you will certainly be doing too much work and delivering too little value.

The Purpose – Ensuring that you have understanding and agreement about what is most important to your client and what it will take to deliver on that. You must establish agreement both on what is most important and on what conditions will satisfy the client that they received the value they need.

Aligning is the stage in which you start talking about action. But you're not interested in any actions unless they're aligned with delivering what is most important to the client. That's your real job here.

STEP FIVE: CLARIFY THE CONDITIONS OF SATISFACTION

Too many times, what people do at this stage is build a specification sheet or an activity list. However, if a client truly trusts you to deliver value and results, they're more trusting about the specifications. People don't fixate on the details of your process unless they're missing clarity about their most important outcomes or don't trust you to take care of their best interests. When you go to a financial planner, do you ask him to explain all the research he's going to do, the resources he uses, or the tools he's going to use to develop your plan? Of course you don't. Even if you did, you probably wouldn't understand what his answers meant.

Now, that doesn't mean you don't clarify the specifications. In order to deliver maximum value, you may need to engage your organization to get important specifications clear. **What is critical is to always recognize that what matters most is not the specifications but the maximization of value, impact, and results. Every part of this step is about aligning your actions, your conversations, your commitments, and your decisions in order to deliver what is most important.**

Clarifying the conditions of satisfaction is about discussing with your client what specifically would satisfy him that his value has been optimally delivered. You are not asking, "Do you want us to do this?" Instead, you are asking, "Would doing this satisfy you that you have the valuable results you need?" **You're getting agreement from the client to be satisfied when they get certain results from your work.** It is far less about meeting every single specification and far more about delivering the greatest impact, value, and results possible.

To understand why this is important, consider the kind of IT projects we've discussed before. In the IT world, statistically, major projects are delivered late more than half the time. If all you're doing is following the specification sheet, you run the risk of upsetting your clients when you deliver anything late. What my high-tech clients have learned to do successfully is clarify the most important results and then maximize the delivery of value by prioritizing and getting those results first. Not every action or specification is of equal value. **What are most valuable are the results that the client needs. You must make sure that everything you do delivers those key results**. That way, if the project is only meeting 80 percent of the specifications, you can still be a hero when you deliver 97 percent of the value and critical functionality on time.

THE VALUE CHAIN PROCESS

The Value Chain Process allows you to validate everything you've done so far and come to a clear and powerful agreement with your client. A powerful agreement means how you'll move forward, gauge success, and deliver the maximum value. Again, this is not about having a huge specification sheet. You need clarity about how to deliver the result, but that's rarely the impediment to success. **The Ultimate Sales Revolution model of success ensures that what is most important and valuable to the client and his organization is what is actually focused on and delivered**. That is the ultimate way to make the client happy and ensure a long and successful relationship.

The Value Chain Process quickly and clearly encapsulates everything you've done, validates it, and gets you to a high-value agreement. The process also ensures that you're dealing with committed, cooperative clients. Once you're enmeshed with a client and have a contract, it is way too late to discover that they're difficult or not going to be satisfied no matter what you do.

After going through the Value Chain Process, you will know whether you're working with a quality client or not. Success in any relationship is a two-way process, so you want a client who is cooperative and committed, especially after you have demonstrated so much impact, value, and goodwill to them. You absolutely want to know if they are going to be good clients as soon as possible.

Here are the three steps of the Value Chain Process:

1) GATHER CLEAR OBJECTIVES

What you know already, because you understand how human beings function, is that **the objectives people toss out, especially early on, are not the objectives that are most important 80 to 90 percent of the time. But it is also important to remember that when people are fixated on an idea or request, you want to have rapport with them and help them get beyond their limited thinking**. This step is about really making sure they've cleared their mind and gotten everything out that they think you need to know.

Get as many objectives, desires, and results out as possible. You're looking for as many meaningful opinions and objectives as you need to build a stepping-stone to the next level. Here are some questions you can ask to get there, of course, done with rapport:

☐ What would you most like to accomplish?

☐ What are your most important, hoped-for results for this quarter or this year?

- [ ] What are the biggest opportunities that you want to take advantage of?

- [ ] What are the biggest challenges you are facing?

- [ ] What are the most important accomplishments that you and your team will be striving for during the time we'll be working together?

2) ESTABLISH MEANINGFUL MEASUREMENTS OF SUCCESS

Here you're talking about meaningful measures of success for the client's business, not necessarily for the objectives they just laid out. This distinction is important because many times the objectives are not what would matter most to their success. Your job is to make sure that you get to the *most meaningful* measurements of success. **The more you can positively affect their business and organization, the more impact and value you have for them.** Make sure you are helping them think as big as possible in what they are measuring.

As an example, when you implement a new set of servers in a client's server farm, there is value to that. But if you help their company improve its financial results and grow their market share with these servers, there is significantly more value in that. When you help their company fulfill its ultimate mission, there is even greater value in that.

You know by now that creating value is your ultimate key to success. **The more meaningful the measurements of success for the client's organization, the greater the impact and value you can offer.** Knowing more about their bigger measurements of success opens additional opportunities as well. Knowing what they need most allows you to increase what you're offering, bringing you more ways to support them. This also expands your openings to work together over a longer term to achieve their really important results.

Either way, you're more valuable to them because with this knowledge you can deliver bigger and better results for them. And it is better for your organization and you when you have bigger opportunities. Now you're talking about *maximizing* your impact, value, and results.

So what are meaningful measurements of success? A lot of people think about things like sales and profit growth or improved retention of their best clients. These are important and valuable outcomes. However, some of the most important metrics are subjective – client satisfaction, employee satisfaction, reputation with clients, perceived value of the brand, how well issues are responded to and fixed, etc. I have taught clients that while these are subjective measurements, when they are measured and monitored regularly they produce an objective trend.

For example, when you are measuring customer satisfaction every six months, by the time you've gotten three measurements, you can see a trend going up or going down. That's an objective trend line using subjective measurements.

Instead of clients saying, "We need more servers," a better measurement of success might be the quantity of profitable services that can be offered to their clients or the speed of implementation of new services. Because more servers offer greater processing capability, it can grow their business with their clients in multiple ways. That's a very meaningful measurement of success. More servers? There is some value in that because it takes some headaches out of the system. However, helping clients increase the offerings by, say, $10 million a year and implement them faster? That's a different value proposition and a much bigger and better one – one that gives you an opening to also talk about other ways you can help them besides just selling them those servers.

Some key questions for this phase of the Value Chain Process, which will help you generate meaningful, measurable metrics of success, include:

☐ What measurements will you use to quantify success?

☐ What are the most important metrics you currently use in your business to quantify progress and success?

☐ How will you know that you have achieved the most important business results that you have committed to for this quarter or this year?

☐ How do these metrics tie to the most critical business results being measured for this quarter or year?

☐ How well are your current measurements of success working for you?

3) DETERMINE THE VALUE WORTH INVESTING IN

The culminating step of the Value Chain Process is establishing, in as concrete ways as possible, that the value of your work with a client warrants their investment. This is only meaningful when you have measurements that matter to work with. **The quality, impact, and significance of achieving their metrics can then be quantified so that the client can see for themself just how valuable these accomplishments would be**. Once again, **a client's determination and articulation of the value is worth multiples more than you telling them what it would be. However, it usually requires your facilitation to help them get there.**

Delivering on the objective of getting high-performing servers that improve speed of processing is definitely worthwhile as an objective, and it would be easy to price that. However, before you ever discuss price, having meaningful measurements of success like expanding your client's offerings to their customers by 25 percent and reducing costs by 15 percent would be far better. **The ultimate level of success, and the step to complete before you really talk price, is to establish in as real and tangible terms as possible what that value would be.**

When you are working with clear measurements, like an expansion of offerings by 25 percent and a reduction of costs by 15 percent, coming up with a real-dollar impact on your client's business is reasonably simple – and compelling. **It is simple to generate a powerful proposal when you can deliver massive return on the investment you are asking your client to make.** The more real and well-quantified it is, the better you have demonstrated the value of this investment.

The key is for your offerings to always be a clear and compelling investment versus being a cost of doing business. If you are selling strategic services, and your client knows your company is known for that, it might be easy to quote a number like $250,000 to deliver your services. That may be acceptable and within their budget. However, what a difference it is to establish meaningful metrics like efficiency improvements in their services, staff productivity improvements, and increases in client retention and satisfaction from your work. That is an even more compelling and higher impact engagement you are forging with the client.

However, the most compelling proposition comes from facilitating so that they can articulate the real impact, value, and results your work can deliver for them. Suppose you can help them establish, on a very conservative basis, that the real-dollar gains are at least $500,000 from staff productivity gains and another $650,000 from improvements in client retention and satisfaction. When your client estimates the value of your work to them at over $1,150,000 in the first year alone, making an investment of $350,000 to accomplish that seems modest and very compelling. While they may have been okay with investing $250,000 for your strategic services based upon your reputation and their objectives, they are likely to be thrilled to engage you for $350,000 to deliver the value that they just surfaced by going through the Value Chain Process.

What I like to say to clients considering buying my professional services is that they must be able to validate at least a 100 percent return on investment the first year to make working together worthwhile. Compare that to the norm, where businesses consider a 25 percent ROI to be outstanding.

Sometimes, the return on investment is subjective, like improved leadership or team effectiveness. Even in those cases, you can start to build metrics to show massive value worth investing in. These could include: reducing the amount of work that has to be redone, increasing the initiative their people show, reducing the amount of time the leader is working on low value projects, and increasing teamwork and collaboration. Metrics that would be useful to track could include: time and expense saved in reducing rework, amount of new projects sold with increased efficiency, real-dollar savings from freeing up 30 percent of the leader's and senior staff's time, savings in personnel costs when people's efficiency goes up, and income from new projects generated through better collaboration and teamwork.

After helping your client come up with measurements like these, it's time to put specific dollar amounts on the value they will get. A good rule of thumb is to have them figure out what they really think that value could be – and then cut it in half. When the value number is really conservative and fair, clients buy in more readily.

When a smart client comes up with – on a conservative basis – you are going to generate over $500,000 of value for them, they will be delighted to pay you a meaningful percentage of the total for that kind of return on investment.

To put it differently, suppose your client says they want leadership training. You say, "That will be $25,000." They might look at you and say that sounds like a lot for leadership development. Instead, suppose you and the client have gone through the Value Chain Process and the client says, "On a very conservative basis, I can see over $500,000 of immediate, added value." Would they then have a problem if you charged $95,000? Probably not. In the context of their return on investment, that's a great ROI. But in the first scenario, charging $25,000 sounded like a lot for the same service.

My company has a client that we worked with for five years doing a training program, which they consistently deemed as one of the most valuable programs they run. The participants documented their individual results, and the numbers were astounding. One day, their SVP came to me and said, "We just came out of a budget meeting, and I just want you to know that you are the most expensive training we run." I said, "Well, that must mean it's the most valuable." She said, "I'm not arguing with you about that. We were just looking at the numbers, and you're the most expensive training."

I said, "You wouldn't spend that money if you didn't get substantial value." She said, "I'm not arguing about that." And the reason she couldn't argue was because we were not just offering training. This client had quantified the results they achieved, and they were getting results that they measured in the tens of millions of dollars from client wins as well as business saved from being lost to competitors. On the basis of that truly extraordinary ROI, it was easy for the client to justify and continue to invest far more in our program. It was not about the program – it was about the exceptional value of their results. (The Ultimate Sales Revolution was the foundation of their program.)

This is simple, really. Consider for yourself what you judge the success of your investments on? You judge them on the value of the return on your investment. **Unless clients see your value, you're an expense**. And when things get tough, expenses get cut. When you're an investment with better than a 100 percent return on that investment, they readily invest.

Questions you can ask to ensure your client is clear about the value worth investing in at this stage include:

- ☐ Are these options consistent with your most important priorities and results?

- ☐ Assuming that you fully achieve these results, what would that be worth to your business (in both measurable, objective terms, and more subjective ways)?

- ☐ When you achieve these results, what kinds of improvements and increases over what you normally expect will they generate?

- ☐ What would it cost your business if you failed to achieve these results?

☐ What are the highest-value results that we should prioritize as our primary focus?

☐ When you are successful, how will this affect your bottom line and overall capabilities as an organization moving forward?

STEP SIX: MAKING MUTUAL COMMITMENTS

In the prior step of the journey to becoming an Indispensable Partner – Clarify the Conditions of Satisfaction – you got your client clear about the value and results they need to be fully satisfied. Your next step is making the mutual commitments with your client to deliver on that understanding. In order to do that, you must plot out what exactly is needed to ensure the client generates the value they need.

Now, mutual commitments are just that – mutual. This is more than what you are going to deliver as the partner and service provider; it also incorporates what the client commits to do to achieve their results. Both parties have an obligation. When clients are talking about hiring you, they may think, "If I'm going to spend 'x' number of dollars with you, then you'd better take care of everything." And many salespeople, in an attempt to curry favor when they don't have the powerful platform of a massive value proposition, will accept that kind of thinking.

Assuring the client that you'll take care of everything, get it done, and the client doesn't need to worry about anything is the antithesis of a high-value partnership. A client willing to abrogate any responsibility for the results is probably a fool. Going along with empty assurances from a salesperson is further proof.

Being clear about your mutual responsibilities is critical for ultimate success. It could be that the client simply needs to be available for review meetings every two weeks, or she needs to sign off when each major benchmark is reached. Whatever it is, the key point is that when you make mutual commitments to each other, it is the foundation for your future relationship together. The commitments you make to each other are critically important because they define the actions you've each committed to take in creating the most valuable and successful relationship possible.

THE INVESTMENT...FINALLY

This is the step where you finally have a conversation about cost. *Not before*. Why wait until this point of the mutual commitment step? Because now the client recognizes the important results she's going to get, the value of making this investment, and the exceptional ROI she will get. You understand the value you're going to provide and what you and your company will get in return. Both sides see the value and agree on it.

As importantly, you've developed a context of trust, respect, and open communication, so when you make commitments together, it is focused on the meaningful results they expect, far more than all those pages of specifications. Your clear facilitation illuminates what matters most, clarifies the most important results, and builds the kind of relationship where the client can trust you to deliver what would be most valuable to her.

Instead of 50+ pages of specifications, this kind of mutual agreement is much shorter and often just a few pages. (However, if you're selling heavily technical solutions, you might have to spell out more specifications.) The framework, or context, of your agreement is:

1. Here are the current conditions that you're dealing with:

2. Here is what you're looking to achieve – the meaningful and measureable results desired:

3. Here is the value of achieving these results:

4. Here are the commitments we're each making in order to achieve these results together:

5. Here is your investment:

Since you have a compelling value proposition, you can call this your client's investment instead of their cost – because it is an investment with a quantified and valuable ROI. Remember the axiom: price is never the issue unless the value isn't clear. **By this point, you've gone through the Value Chain Process, and the value of the results they can expect are crystal clear, quantified, agreed to, and a basis upon which you can build an ongoing, sustainable, and exceptionally valuable relationship.** This is about being the kind of Indispensable Partner in their success that has them wanting to make an investment in you! That's why price is not an issue. This is about a mutual investment being made in this relationship to achieve valuable results.

HANDLING CHANGES

The power of the Ultimate Sales Revolution process is that once you've made mutual commitments together, it marks the basis for your ongoing work together building your Indispensable Partner relationship.

For example, in any major project, or even minor projects, changes are going to happen. The unforeseen shows up, the marketplace changes, the demands change, people change, budgets change. The point is: change happens. Most of the time when change happens, people get reactive. In today's world, you must be able to adapt to change. **Here is the power of making mutual commitments and understanding what is most valuable: It gives you clarity and a foundation to negotiate the changes in your agreement.**

Suppose you and your client need to decide whether some of the specifications have changed. The conversation starts with: "Are you trying to get the same important results, or have the valuable outcomes we agreed to changed?" If the high-value outcomes have changed, you need to renegotiate your commitments to each other. You can go back to the previous step of Clarifying the Conditions of Satisfaction and go through the Value Chain Process so you're clear about what really has to be renegotiated. This saves you from becoming like the company I told you about that finished a three-year, $8 million dollar project and then had it trashed.

Remember the other story I told about the $500 million company with $8 million of questionable collections? That mostly happened because when something had to change in a project, rather than getting a formal change agreement, their people said to their clients, "Don't worry about it. Let's just do this, and we'll figure it out in the end." In reality, it was their people trying to buy trust and relationship, rather than building it via the Indispensable Partner process.

However, when the undocumented addition to the bill came at the end of a project, the clients protested. Teaching their people how to build Indispensable Partner relationships with their clients gave them the principles, practices, and skills for a constructive, value-focused renegotiation of commitments. Using these skills, they shrunk those questionable collections considerably. Over the next four years they more than doubled the size of their business, while reducing questionable collections to under $2,000,000 – an eight-fold improvement, based on these superior relationship-building practices.

When changes occur, you must be clear about what has changed and how that change affects the results, the commitments, and the relationship. That is how you make change a friend in strengthening your relationships rather than a feared situation to be avoided.

What the Indispensable Partner process does is build a holistic environment that is held together by our relationship and commitments to each other. It is much like a marriage – a professional marriage. **You need to ensure that your commitment to the success of the relationship transcends challenges, issues, changes, or anything else that happens in your day-to-day world.** This process provides the framework for constantly monitoring the health and well-being of your relationship and agreements. If something changes, you're in a good position to identify it and deal with it constructively.

Once you get competent at this, you can go through the Indispensable Partner process with your clients very quickly. When you have your attention focused on them, with rapport and an understanding of what they value, the conversation can become as fast as this:

You: "How are you doing?"

Client: "Great. Happy to see you."

You: "Happy to see you too. Any major changes since we last talked?"

Client: "No, we're still on track."

You: "Fantastic."

That's the way it goes with your best clients. You have gone through every step of the process in seconds because of the quality of your relationship. Of course, your most challenging client conversations look nothing like this at all.

However, something like this might happen (and it did happen with a client once):

You: "Any major changes since we last talked?

Client: "Yeah. Somebody bought us yesterday."

That's a profound change of circumstances. So let's go back to the process. You have rapport with your client. You are focused on your client's best interests, and they know you're there to serve their best interests. So you can go back to step three, Revealing the Client's Concerns: "What does that mean for you? What does it mean for the organization? What does it mean for the projects we're working on?"

Now we're revealing their concerns and how they might affect the value-based agreements you are working on. "Okay, what is most important given where you are now? What have the leaders said about what is critical for these projects?" And you follow the process, building from there back to making new mutual commitments if needed.

PUTTING IDEAS INTO PRACTICE

TEST YOURSELF: HANDLING TOUGH
BUSINESS SITUATIONS

Go back to the challenging relationship you identified earlier. How would you approach it and handle it differently using all the principles, practices, and skills you've learned?

What was missing that made this situation and relationship difficult or challenging?

How can you approach this differently to be far more effective?

What Indispensable Partner principles and skills would you employ?

CHAPTER EIGHT

GROWING YOUR IMPACT, VALUE, AND SUCCESS

"Every time you are tempted to react in the same old way, ask if you want to be a prisoner of the past or a pioneer of the future."

—DEEPAK CHOPRA

Now that you've learned about the Ultimate Sales Revolution principles and practices, it is important to **remember that the whole process, when done well, is a fluid, highly integrated, dynamic process. Every step is built on the foundation of the prior step. That means that if you're having difficulty at any step of the process, you need to go back one step to ensure that the prior step is strong and well established**.

For example, maximizing client value is Step Four. If you don't know their concerns, it is hard to get to that level of value. If you're not getting strong opinions to reveal their concerns, then you must go back and make sure you have rapport. If you cannot seem to establish rapport, you have to make sure you're really present and focused on the client and they understand you're there for them.

Integrating each step of the process is critical, and you must employ each step in the order in which they've been presented. Remember that once you become highly skilled at this and you've built a tremendous relationship with a client, you can cover the steps in seconds. When you have a quality relationship with somebody, you're there with them, you've got great rapport, and the questions come easily: How are you doing? What's been happening? Has anything changed since we talked last?

The delivery of value is built on the quality of the relationship. And the relationship is built on the quality of communication. This process is really built on three basic foundations – communication, relationship building, and the generation of value.

The reason this works so well is because this is how human beings actually function. The problem for many people is that work has gotten away from being a source of deep meaning and creative expression. It has become too much about a paycheck, and too many salespeople operate like that. These folks – and their clients – are the ones who need the Sales Exorcism to clean up and get rid of those negative sales practices.

Done well, sales is about creating extraordinarily successful relationships. With this approach you will not only be far more successful, but the level of enjoyment in your work relationships will also be significantly greater.

The best-of-the-best, most successful salespeople approach every client with integrity, demonstrating they can be trusted and provide massive value to their clients. They build deep bonds and relationships as they produce exceptional impact, value, and results for their clients and their companies. This can be done with virtually anybody – if you understand and effectively apply these principles. What kind of difference, in every meaningful dimension, would that make for you?

IMPROVING YOUR BEST AND YOUR MOST CHALLENGING CLIENT RELATIONSHIPS

All along you've been asked to consider your best and most challenging clients in the context of what you've been learning. One of the reasons you keep looking at your best and most challenging clients is because your own experience should validate every principle of this process. You can see why it is so powerful to apply universal human dynamics.

To really understand the universality and impeccability of this process, please go back and consider how these relationships got to be the way they are, based on these principles you've learned. For example, with your best clients you surely have good rapport. With your most difficult clients you are probably a bit intimidated (a nasty form of preoccupation), don't have good rapport, and don't have a clue what their most important objectives and results would be. It is not surprising that they are challenging clients!

At this point, using what you have learned, consider ways to improve all of your key relationships. This is just as important with your good clients, because you can often turn a good client into a great client, one that you can influence on a higher level of value and whose relationship lasts for many years to come. You can also turn around your challenging relationships when you apply these principles and practices well.

CHAPTER NINE

KILLING SALES MYTHS AND ADDITIONAL RESOURCES

"Talent hits the target others cannot hit.
Genius hits a target that others cannot see."

—ARTHUR SCHOPENHAUER

KILLING 7 NASTY MYTHS OF SELLING

Here are some of the most common – and nasty – myths of sales and how they reduce your effectiveness. Understanding these as trap doors to difficulty and away from the elevator to superior success reinforces the critical need to practice the Ultimate Sales Revolution principles. Your greatest success comes when you abandon old, ineffective ways of thinking about and practicing sales, upgrade your effectiveness, and become an Indispensable Partner in your clients' success.

MYTH #1: "I JUST NEED TO PROBE A LITTLE MORE."

This kind of thinking is all about what a salesperson is going to do to a client. Too many people, especially salespeople, are taught that this is the way to improve communications. I always ask students and clients this common sense question: "How many of you like to be probed?" No one does. It is the same with other things sales-people do to their clients, like, "I need to close them." Who likes to be closed, especially in the context of a high-value relationship? No one does. The close is about the salesperson's perspective on the deal, not creating value in the relationship. The Ultimate Sales Revolution focuses on the relationship, because, done well, that creates massive mutual success.

MYTH #2: "I NEED TO GET THEM IN TOUCH WITH THEIR PAIN."

There are whole schools of selling about getting clients in touch with their pain. I think that approaching people as if what is wrong is the best place to operate falls into that manipulative area most clients hate. Even if we agree that people make decisions for two reasons – to avoid pain and to maximize pleasure – a pain-focused approach leaves out half the people and the motivation the best have for being outstanding. The most successful sales-people recognize that clients' greatest opportunities are at least as important a decision maker as their biggest challenges. The "going for pain" process is about driving a client where your tech-niques orient you. This kind of manipulative, salesperson-driven technique is indicative of a limited capacity for building outstand-ing relationships.

MYTH #3: "I JUST NEED A BETTER ELEVATOR SPEECH."

To which I always say, "If you can explain your value in an elevator speech, it is trivial value." What you really want to have is a con-versation where you engage someone in such a way that they want to know more about you and the value you could have for them.

You don't need an elevator speech; you want a value-generating engagement dialogue. Furthermore, it's really not about you; it's about them and what would be important and valuable to them.

Below are some examples of context setting and engaging openings to create a dialogue when you are selling high-end professional services. Note that in each instance, the key to developing a dialogue is to set an engaging context and ask a question that turns the conversation back to them. Here is how you could answer when someone asks, "What do you do?"

- ☐ We help clients accelerate the achievement of their most critical results. Do you have important and valuable projects that you know could be done better and faster? What do you think are the most critical factors that would increase the results?

- ☐ We work with clients to bring strategic alignment to their executive teams to accelerate their most critical results. How well aligned and focused are all of your key executives on achieving the company's most important objectives? If it is not at 100 percent, what is missing to make that happen?

- ☐ We work with clients to build the leadership and communication skills that make them the top performers in their industry. How effective and successful is the leadership and communication in your organization? What would make it even more successful?

MYTH #4: "I JUST NEED TO BE BETTER AT EXPLAINING WHAT I DO."

Smart clients and prospects don't want to hear what you do nor really care what you do. It is not about you. Even if they ask you, "What do you do?" that's shorthand for, "What do you do that would be extremely valuable and meaningful for me?" The second part of that question is their real interest. The more you talk about you and what you do, the more you are missing the chance to have the impact you and they are really looking for. People want to know the value they are going to get out of the relationship.

This also raises the issue of getting you away from being the focus of the conversation. Being a facilitator of what is most important to them demonstrates that you can be a valuable partner in their success. Your ability to facilitate their clarity and focus on what matters most to them is a far-superior demonstration of your value than anything that you can say about who you are and what you do.

MYTH #5: "THE KEY TO GETTING PAID WELL IS TO NEGOTIATE BETTER."

What you've learned in this book is not negotiation skills. This is beyond negotiation skills. One corporate client put more than 1,200 of their people through an earlier version of this program. Partway through, they realized that more than half of the participants had already taken the negotiation course that had been in the curriculum for years. However, you couldn't tell that they had any negotiation skills when they were going through our program.

On the other hand, a quarter of their people attended our program first and then went to the negotiation course after learning to become an Indispensable Partner using the Ultimate

Sales Revolution skills. Those people were notable superstars in the negotiation course. They knew how to communicate, develop a value proposition, and get to what was most important to the other person. Too often in negotiation – and in old-school sales – salespeople are constructing a position that enables them to get what they want. However, you get your greatest rewards when you facilitate what is most important to your clients and maximize the impact, value, and results they really need.

MYTH #6: "I JUST NEED TO EXPLAIN MY VALUE BETTER."

Once again, this approach fails because it is about you and not them. You must start by being focused and clear about what is really most important to them. You don't need more explanations when your way of communicating and building the trust, respect, and open communication helps them see your value. Your real job is helping them clarify, articulate, and understand the value that is most important to them. Getting them to see and articulate the value they need is far more powerful than explaining what you think your value is. Remember the axiom: it is at least ten times more powerful for you to help them clarify what is most important and understand the value than for you to tell them what the value is.

There is a truism about influence that comes into play here: People don't argue with their own data. What someone gets clear about, understands the value of, and defines the value of for herself will be many multiples more compelling than the same information spoken by you. Remember, the power of facilitating clarity with your clients has significantly more impact and value than what you might tell them – even if you are absolutely right. That is basic human nature.

MYTH #7: "I DID EXACTLY WHAT THEY ASKED ME TO, AND THEY'RE STILL NOT HAPPY."

Remember the story of the three-year, $8 million project that got thrown in the trash. It doesn't make any difference if you did what they asked. It only makes a difference if you delivered the value they really needed.

Everything about the Ultimate Sales Revolution is designed to give you the principles, practices, and skills to create real, meaningful value with every client. Doing what someone – even an important client – asks you to do means you are not delivering maximum value 80 to 90 percent of the time. You already know you start with a gap in trust between many clients and salespeople – even if you are a fully trustworthy partner. Doing what someone asks is not high-level proof of your ability to work with them. Too often, it positions you as an order taker, ranking in position below your buyer.

The most dramatic testimonial to your value as a trusted, worthy, and equal partner in your client's success is facilitating their clarity and focus on what really matters and is worth doing. **Saving a client from making a poor or low-value decision is one of the most dramatic ways to clearly demonstrate your value and impact**. As a trusted partner in their success, your real job is to facilitate clarity about what is most important and valuable to the clients. Doing anything else diminishes your value and standing as the partner your client should work with.

ULTIMATE SALES REVOLUTION AXIOMS

Here are ten additional, favorite success principles. You can get more insights and information about these by going to our website at www.InstituteForSalesInnovation.com/videos.

THE FIRST LAW OF SUCCESS:

Distinguish what you do that works –
Do more of that.
Distinguish what you do that doesn't work –
Do less of that.
The ultimate key to success is being able to make the distinctions.

MINDSET + ACTION = RESULTS

There are two high-impact keys to
successfully improving your results –
You change what you are doing, or
you change how you think about it.
The obvious challenge in changing actions is
the major impediment to change: your habits.

WHAT IS YOUR
REAL JOB?

As a top professional, your real job – regardless of your position – is to be a facilitator of what is most important to your clients. Anything else is a misunderstanding of your responsibilities and limits your success.

CLARITY OF
WHAT AND WHY
ALWAYS BEFORE
HOW

You must always be clear about WHAT is most important and
WHY that is the best possible choice of what is most important
before you begin to work on HOW to do it.

THE 50 CHOICES PARADOX

I ask every top executive and professional to choose
one of these options:
You have 50 things on your to do list.
You can choose to act on priorities 1, 2, and 3, or you can choose
priorities 4 to 50. You can choose one but never touch the other.
You know that common sense is choosing priorities 1, 2, and 3.
However, all too often, that is not common practice.
When common sense becomes common practice – amazing and
remarkable results show up!

FOCUSING ON WHAT IS MOST IMPORTANT
IS THE FUNDAMENTAL FULCRUM FOR
LEVERAGE IN DECISION-MAKING – AND WITH
EVERYONE YOU WANT TO INFLUENCE

Poor decision-making and results
comes from focusing on issues other than what really matters.
Highly effective decision making always
takes account of what is most important.

THE VALUE VERSUS ACTIVITY
DECISION-MAKING GRID

Clarity of value should always drive the choice of activities.
Otherwise, there will be way too much activity
with way too little value generated.

PRICE IS NEVER THE ISSUE –
UNLESS THE VALUE IS NOT CLEAR

When clients do not perceive the value equation, they are more
likely to be fixated on the price.
The only way to diminish the attention on price is to move the
focus to the value the client is getting.

RESULTS ARE ALWAYS WORTH MULTIPLES OF THE
VALUE THAT ACTIVITIES OR PROCESSES PROVIDE.

Always focus on selling the value of your results.
Make sure you always know
what the building blocks for success are.
Clear and compelling components of your
equation means greater likelihood of real success.

ESTABLISHING 'EQUATIONS FOR SUCCESS'

The simpler and more valuable the variables are, the more
powerful and compelling the equation is to clients.

TROUBLESHOOTING GUIDE

These are some of the typical situations that challenge even successful salespeople. What follows are ways to correct the limitations and issues that are likely causing the problem by using the principles, practices, and skills of the Ultimate Sales Revolution.

ISSUE A: "I CAN'T GET AN APPOINTMENT WITH THIS PROSPECT."

To someone having this problem, the first question is, what are you asking for? If you're asking, "Can I get ten minutes to discuss our services," then why would somebody want to see you? This is a request for your benefit, without a clear and compelling value proposition for them.

Instead, what you really need to start with is a meaningful-to-them context-setting comment. You also need to make sure you have rapport. You're probably getting voicemail, so you know how fast this person talks. You want to match and mirror their speaking to help you build rapport with your context-setting message.

You always need to start with their concerns. Have you done your research to understand their concerns? Suppose you've read that the company just went through a merger. You can use that information to look at their concerns and ask something like, "Would it be valuable to look at how to get the cultures working together as fast as possible?" If your research shows they've got a big budget for IT expenditures, you might ask, "Mr. CIO, would it be valuable to review options on how you can maximize the effectiveness and impact of your budget?" You're not asking for time for you. You're asking them to consider valuable options that would help them.

Note the lack of "I," "me," and "we" in those questions. **As much as possible, you want to take I, me, and we out of your conversation** – then watch what happens. Starting with, "I'd like to get an appointment with you," says it is going to be about you. "When would be a good time to look at ways to improve the effectiveness and results of your salesforce?" says you are about valuable outcomes for them. You must look at what would be valuable enough for the prospect to want to give you an appointment. That's a very different way of thinking.

ISSUE B: "IT ALWAYS COMES DOWN TO WHAT OUR PRICE IS."

It is highly premature to name a price before you have gone through a value-clarifying and quantifying process. If you do, you are creating an obstacle where there is a very high probability that you will not get the deal and certainly not at the price you quote.

Why? Any price sounds like too much unless there is a substantial context of value behind it. It makes no difference what you are selling, how much it costs, or anything else unless there is a context of value to the person who has to deal with your price.

The answer that I give to anybody who calls me up and asks, "How much would it cost to have you speak, do a training, or facilitate our team?" is, "What are you trying to accomplish with this presentation/training/facilitation that would be most valuable for your group?" The conversation is all about them and their valuable result.

When somebody asks me, "What do you include in your educational programs?" my first question is, "What are the most important results you're working to create through the training?" It is always critical to establish the results and the value to the buyer, their organization, and their clients before ever quoting any price. Then you can be evaluated by the value you can deliver rather than the price you are charging.

ISSUE C: "THE CLIENT IS HAPPY WITH THEIR CURRENT VENDOR AND ISN'T LOOKING FOR SOMEBODY NEW."

When a client or prospect tells you something like this, you can either fight them, or you can use the Ultimate Sales Revolution process. What is the key to success? Start by engaging them in a relationship with rapport.

Your response to your prospect could be, "That's outstanding – and very unusual. What do you like most about how they take care of you?" You're not disputing what they're saying or trying to convince them they should work with you. And you're not walking away because they said they're perfectly happy. You're working to create value and clarity for them in the same way you do for everybody. Note the use of superlatives to get to highly distilled thinking quickly. The conversation would go this way:

You: "What do you like most about them?"

Prospect: "They're always on time, and the quality is always high."

You: "What else do you like most about them?"

Prospect: "Well, they show up when I call, and they're always responsive when I've got a need."

You: "Is there anything else that you like as much as that?"

Prospect: "Well, there might be one or two others."

> You: "Is there anything else they do well but maybe not as perfectly?"
>
> Prospect: "Well, yeah, a couple things. Sometimes I have to talk to them three or four times in order to get something clear because the sales support people just goofed up something."
>
> You: "Is there anything else that's okay but not as great as these other things that you like so much?"
>
> Prospect: "Sometimes they'll give my assistant a hard time. They like talking to me, but sometimes I'm busy or I just shouldn't be handling certain things."

What just happened? The prospect has told you both what they value most and showed you where the gap is. The question now is, "What does it mean to you when they don't treat your assistant well? What's the impact when you've got to make three or four calls to get something done that really should be simple?"

> Prospect: "Well, we move fast here, and I get frustrated at times when things take up more of my time than they need to."
>
> You: "How open would you be to considering a resource who could do the four things you love most *and* eliminate these two headaches for you?"

This is a prime example of using the questioning strategy outlined in Chapter 6. Get an opinion. Find out what it represents. When your client says, "I'm perfectly happy with my current vendor," is that a fact or opinion? Obviously it's an opinion. It's a strong opinion, which means you can get to what matters most to him using the process. You're not telling him why you're better than his current vendor. And you didn't fight or disagree with him to get there. You didn't start defending your position, which is what many people do when they hit a wall.

As with all successful relationship building, you start with rapport, keep the focus on the prospect, and use questions to find out what was most important to her. Even if she isn't ready to change vendors right now, at the very least you've established yourself as someone she'll remember – and consider.

ISSUE D: "THE PROSPECTS SAY THEY LOVE WHAT YOU DO, BUT THEY DON'T HAVE THE BUDGET."

Budget is one of the worst excuses ever because people get fixed on budgets as a rigid spending plan. **Smart leaders treat budgets as an allocation of resources to achieve their most important results.** When you help somebody get clear about their most important result, but they claim budget woes, you may need to help them get clear about how to make better decisions with their budgets.

Prospect: "This is a great solution to a really critical priority, but we don't have any budget."

You: "Would this solution be one of your top three to five priorities?"

Prospect: "Oh yeah, absolutely. One of the top five initiatives we should be working on."

You: "Are you open to some very powerful decision-making consulting for free?"

Prospect: "Sure."

You: "If you're spending money on things that aren't your most important priorities and not allocating your funds to achieve your top priorities – that's ineffective decision making. (*Take a pause to let that sink in.*) What you may want to do is reallocate your budget, moving money away from less important projects and putting funds toward achieving what is most important to your organization. Otherwise, you're going to achieve less important goals rather than your top priorities. How successful do you think that is going to be?"

That's a pretty bold way to talk to a prospect, but what has just been proven? Number one, that you understand his top priorities, and he does too. Number two, that good decision making is all about focusing on the top priorities. And number three, that you would be an honest and effective partner for him and his important results.

For more troubleshooting scenarios, visit our websites:

- ☐ www.InstituteForSalesInnovation.com for sales and sales leadership insights and resources

- ☐ www.OptimizeIntl.com for leadership and executive team coaching and development content and resources

ABOUT THE INSTITUTE FOR SALES INNOVATION AND OPTIMIZE INTERNATIONAL

"The greatest danger for most of us is not that our aim is too high and we miss it, but that it is too low and we reach it."

—MICHELANGELO

We are dedicated to our clients receiving the highest-impact sales and leadership coaching, development, and education. Clients are supported in developing the most successful influencers, sales professionals, leaders, and managers who are passionate about profoundly inspiring, impacting, and improving the impact, value, results, and success of their people, organization, and clients.

Clients become outstanding at accelerating and expanding their clients' and their own growth and results. They become adept at reaching their highest levels of accomplishment using The Ultimate Sales Revolution principles and practices. Our clients excel at becoming Indispensable Partners in the success of their key customers. Our passion is working with clients to ensure the acceleration, fulfillment, and accomplishment of their vision, mission, and most important goals.

Our clients' success is based on four core deliverables we partner with them to achieve:

☐ Increasing sales results by becoming the best value-generating, Indispensable Partner with every critical constituency – their clients, colleagues, company, community, and everyone else that affects the success of their business.

☐ Facilitating the creation of a high-performing, collaborative culture, where passion and personal fulfillment are encouraged to accelerate and increase the most meaningful, high-impact contributions and organizational results.

☐ Enabling synergies among leaders and their teams to deliver extraordinary and valuable impact and results.

☐ Developing executive teams into powerful, results-driven leaders who are respected and supported by their peers, and eagerly followed by their people.

For more information, visit our websites at:
www.InstituteForSalesInnovation.com
and www.OptimizeIntl.com,
or call 978-369-4525.

ACKNOWLEDGEMENTS

This book is a labor of love and passion, and the support, guidance, insight, and love of so many people over many years have made this possible. I honor all of the people who have taught, mentored, and challenged me, as well as those who have allowed me to do the same with them. What follows is but a partial list of those to whom I am indebted, and who are a part of bringing this book and work to you.

The biggest thank you possible to my wife Terri for your generosity of spirit, willingness to tolerate and be amused by my challenging boundaries and limitations, and whose love and support is a daily reminder of how much is possible in a great relationship. My children Julie, Jenn, Dave, and Harry are a never-ending source of love, inspiration, and blessings, as well as a constant reminder of how much is possible in contributing to making a better world.

Nothing has expanded my vision, enhanced my insights, and elevated my thinking more than the great masters and mentors I have had the amazing great fortune to study deeply with and learn much from. These are people who have expanded what is possible in the world, not just for me, but for many. They include the great masters of their fields Dr. James Tin Yan So, Fernando Flores, Stuart Heller, and Tony Robbins. The spiritual blessings and guidance of Baba Muktananda and Gurumayi Chidvilasananda are profound beyond words. I am forever grateful for the guidance of the great mentors in my life: Ted Edwards, Sr, Alan Weiss, and Brendon Burchard. They have challenged me to grow and provided direct, incisive lessons I needed at different points in my journey.

So many clients over the years have provided great opportunities for my learning and growth as I sought to deliver the same to them. I am forever grateful to all of my clients for the gift of your trust, respect, openness, and demand for better ways to work, live, and contribute, which has challenged me to grow and develop myself to serve you better. I must recognize a few for their special impact on my thinking, development, and career: Tony Candito, Greg Ross, and Jack Sullivan; Nancy Stager and Rich Holbrook; Marcia Mendes d'Abrue; Cynthia Carpenter; Basil Denno; and Jim Cowden. What makes them so special as leaders, clients, and people is their level of integrity, continual commitment to excellence, intellectual curiosity, openness to finding new and better ways even when they were already so successful in their fields, and passionate desire to be outstanding leaders and contributors in service of their people and clients. You have each touched me deeply, and inspired me to new heights.

One of the great gifts in my life has been the opportunity to have my friends become my colleagues, and my colleagues become my friends. My dear friends and masterminding partners Mitchell Stevko and Judi Spear have been priceless additions to my life and work. A special thank you to my always dear friends and sometimes collaborators Thomas Benton, Meredith Kimbell, Jane Deuber, and Ted Edwards, Jr. To my oldest friends and partners in the journey of life Justin Fallon, Ron Bernstein, Jeremy Seligman and Rich Margil, from whom I continue to learn and be inspired, I treasure the friendship and engagement we have been so fortunate to share over the years.

I offer a big thank you to my editing, design and publication team at Advantage Media Group, who have set standards for caring and responsiveness, and been a joy to work with.

To all of you who share the passion for high quality professional relationships that create real value and impact, and make the world a better and more meaningful place to be – may this book accelerate and expand your journey and success!